BREAKING
→THE←
BOSS
BIAS

Walkley Award–winning journalist Catherine Fox spent two decades at the *Financial Review*, writing the popular Corporate Woman column, and has consulted to many of Australia's largest organisations, including the ADF. She is the author of *Better than Sex* (with Helen Trinca), *Women Kind* (with Kirstin Ferguson), *The F Word* (with Jane Caro), *7 Myths about Women and Work* and *Stop Fixing Women*. In 2022 she was made a member of the Order of Australia for services to journalism and gender equity.

'Forensically researched, tightly argued, suffused with Fox's trademark wit, *Breaking the Boss Bias* presents a compelling case for more women leaders and asks the question – why are they still so rare?'

Jane Caro

'What a wake-up call! We are moving backwards on gender, and the stats for women who come from diverse backgrounds are staggering. This is compulsory reading for all leaders.'

Shirley Chowdhary

'No matter what they do or how high they fly, most women know what it feels like to be ignored or left out of decision making. Instead of being fobbed off with excuses, this important and practical book outlines why it happens and what we can all do about it.'

Melissa Doyle AM

'This book isn't just about women but about building a better future for everyone. A powerful and important book for our times and must-read for all leaders.'

Kirstin Ferguson AM

'This meticulously researched case for change is exactly what we need to move us from incrementally playing around the edges to sustainable, systemic progress towards gender equality in leadership.'

Michelle Ryan

'Catherine cuts through the crippling stereotypes, exposes backlash and bias, delivers disruption and serves up seven steps for real change. She has proven to be Australia's corporate gender equality whisperer.'

Natasha Stott Despoja AO

BREAKING
→ THE ←
BOSS
BIAS

How to get more women
into leadership

CATHERINE FOX

NEWSOUTH

UNSW Press acknowledges the Bedegal people, the Traditional Owners of the unceded territory on which the Randwick and Kensington campuses of UNSW are situated, and recognises the continuing connection to Country and culture. We pay our respects to Bedegal Elders past and present.

A NewSouth book

Published by
NewSouth Publishing
University of New South Wales Press Ltd
University of New South Wales
Sydney NSW 2052
AUSTRALIA
https://unsw.press/

© Catherine Fox 2024

10 9 8 7 6 5 4 3 2 1

National Library of Australia
Cataloguing-in-Publication entry

A catalogue record for this book is available from the National Library of Australia

ISBN   9781742238197 (paperback)
            9781742239033 (ebook)
            9781761178009 (ePDF)

Internal design Josephine Pajor-Markus
Cover design Alissa Dinallo
Printer Griffin Press

All reasonable efforts were taken to obtain permission to use copyright material reproduced in this book, but in some cases copyright could not be traced. The author welcomes information in this regard.

This book is printed on paper using fibre supplied from plantation or sustainably managed forests.

Women belong in all places where decisions are being made.

—*Ruth Bader Ginsburg*

Contents

Introduction   1

1   Replacing over-optimism with reality and action   7

2   Breaking down the bias barriers   34

3   Tackling the elephant in the room: Backlash   64

4   Learning new leadership lessons   94

5   Addressing everyday sexism   123

6   Leading differently: Disrupting jobs, careers
    and power structures   151

7   Elevating decisive women   184

The end of delusions   210

Notes   215

Bibliography   225

Index   226

Introduction

In recent years a group of remarkable Australian women has hit the news, finally stepping into some top jobs running organisations, and being elected to federal parliament in record numbers. Overdue changes, such as introducing paid parental leave, have also seen more women stay in the workforce, and they continue to be better educated, on average, than men.

Despite these factors, the evidence reveals a sobering reality: women remain very much on the sidelines or absent in many key decision-making groups.

Change has been painfully slow and inconsistent. The overwhelming majority of decision-makers – CEOs, chairs, government leaders and senior executives – are still men. Women are nowhere near having an equal say in how businesses, government and society run.

A few decades in journalism and advocacy for women's rights have helped me develop a well-tuned detector for exaggerated claims about women marching into power. Delving into the data shows a different picture from the sophisticated gender washing by organisations, and trumpeting of small improvements in statistics. The convenient fiction that the 'gender problem' isn't really a problem anymore (sometimes called the 'progress narrative') has flourished.

Worryingly, this handily disguises the problem, and undermines the need for advocacy and action. As the following chapters make clear, I think it's time to ring the alarm bells or risk reversing even the small advances made in recent decades.

The case for change I've set out shows there's a pressing need to tackle the significant levels of bias and sexism that buffer men and stymie women; progress towards equity is not linear or assured; and in particular, the incremental shift that saw more women move into authority has plateaued or even deteriorated. That matters for all of us because critical decisions are being around the world without women at the table.

International data shows the leadership gender gap has widened. For the past eight years, the proportion of women hired into leadership positions has been steadily increasing by about 1 per cent per year globally, according to the 2023 Global Gender Gap Index, a snapshot and ranking of international progress towards equity.[1] But this sluggish trend shows a clear reversal starting in 2022, which brings the 2023 rate back to 2021 levels.

Internationally, the shocking treatment of women and girls reveals the outcomes from this lack of power. This includes the appalling banning of girls from school in Afghanistan, and poisoning them when they attend in Iran. It also reflects what's happening to women in the US, since the Supreme Court overturned *Roe v Wade*, the constitutional right to abortion, leaving many women unable to make decisions about their own bodies. Women are often missing from senior climate change forums, as government leaders and in powerful financial roles. Camouflaging these failures as a minor ripple while a tide of change sweeps us all ahead is disingenuous and distracts us from the urgent need for action, not apathy, in every country.

If there's been little change at the top, there's not been much in the kitchen either. Women in Australia do two-thirds of caring and domestic work, and picked up an extra hour a day of unpaid work during the pandemic. They're even cooking more meals. Instead of the cooking gender gap shrinking, as it had for the three years up to 2022, it widened around the world.[2] Gendered violence in Australia has reached horrific levels, with more women killed in the first few months of 2024 than the previous year, triggering calls for urgent action.

This bleak picture, exacerbated by the COVID years, and the dangerous idea that gender equity had been 'fixed', were key reasons I felt compelled to write this book now. I realised that efforts to get more women into power shouldn't be seen as a sidebar to the fight for equity. They are urgently needed to beat the sexism holding all women back. I've seen the robust data showing that when women are at the top table, they help set different agendas, and are more likely to prioritise and support gender equity. They motivate and inspire younger women. At the same time, it's become more obvious to me that forcing women to conform to a masculine version of leadership is not the answer. Redefining who can be the boss and what leadership looks like is essential, and depend on opening the door to let in new contenders, both in quantity and quality.

This book maps out seven interconnected ways to break the latest wave of boss bias keeping women out of power. The first four chapters focus on identifying key barriers and the following chapters outline how to address them:

1   Replacing over-optimism with reality and action
    How denial and gender washing is holding back progress
2   Breaking down the bias barriers
    Navigating the sexism that still derails mothers and all
    women aspiring to leadership
3   Tackling the elephant in the room: Backlash
    Coming to grips with increasing resistance to gender equity
4   Learning new leadership lessons
    Reshaping the male leadership default in business
    teaching, case studies and media
5   Addressing everyday sexism
    The best ways to deal with micro-aggressions
6   Leading differently: Disrupting jobs, careers and
    power structures
    How smart leaders are breaking bias and setting
    a new norm
7   Elevating decisive women
    Recognising the skills and contributions of women
    decision-makers

While this analysis is confronting at times, there's a hefty dose of optimism, too. Australia has an opportunity to take up the change from some key steps forward: there's more generous paid parental leave, and growing support for men to use it; a shift in recognition of sexual harassment and victim blaming and the need to address intersectionality; the launch of Respect at Work legislation on the back of a comprehensive review; the Women's Economic Equality Taskforce recommendations; and the introduction of publicly published gender pay gaps for employers reporting to the Workplace Gender Equality Agency. It's a solid platform to build on.

The reasons for urgent action on gender quality have never been more obvious, as I demonstrate throughout this book. And the rising tide lifts all boats: there's a massive upside across society in tackling gender bias now and into the future. Dismantling rigid gender norms would add about $128 billion annually to the Australian economy, according to Deloitte Access Economics and Australians Investing in Women.[3] Many Australians are increasingly recognising the benefits of women leaders. In late 2023, a poll found the most popular Australian politicians were three women: Foreign Minister Penny Wong; former Defence employee Jacquie Lambie; and Senator Jacinta Price. Pressure is also growing from a younger and diverse generation who expect to see leaders who look like them.

My main focus, and what I know best, is the dynamics in business and formal workplaces, but I have also used a range of input from community, not-for-profit, small business and government, too. And I've included the experiences of women who face the kinds of intersectional barriers I have not had to face myself, such as racism, disability bias and homophobia. While I have quoted gender workforce and leadership statistics, there is a significant lack of data on women from marginalised cohorts, such as Indigenous and non-Anglo women, women with disabilities and from the LGBTIQ+ community, which is urgently needed to address the additional bias barriers they face.

A word about language. The description 'woman' includes anyone who identifies as such. I've also often substituted 'decision-making' for 'leadership', which automatically conjures up an image of a white bloke in a suit sitting in the corner office.

The many women I spoke to are hopeful but realistic enough to know that much more has to be done to have their concerns taken seriously. 'I think there's a huge burn-out of trust for women in this country', former Australia Post CEO Christine Holgate told me.[4] Attacked in parliament for giving some executives luxury watches as a bonus, she was mocked and widely criticised, before losing her job. She said there was no way a man in her position would have been treated with such contempt. But she stood up for herself in public, and received thousands of supportive messages from women. They recognised the bullying behaviour and the impact when a woman is at the table to take up these issues. We've been too polite and don't talk about it, she told me, but I'm not polite anymore.

I'm not either. I'm fed up with being told the problem is being solved and women are now treated the same as men. They're not. I've trawled the research, interviewed the experts, talked to hundreds of women, and spent decades examining the best ways to break the bias holding us back. I know a pattern when I see one – the closer we get to power, the more resistance we meet. But women in Australia are also better educated and more vocal than ever. Here's the latest evidence and tactics to cut through the noise and motivate us all to finally break the boss bias.

Chapter 1
Replacing over-optimism with reality and action

It felt like 2023 was shaping up to be a watershed year for women. Record audiences tuned in to the Women's World Cup (WWC); the *Barbie* movie became one of the top grossing movies ever made; and pop singer Taylor Swift was named *Time* magazine's Person of the Year. Hearing patriarchy turn up in conversations, while millions were watching teams like the Matildas in full flight, scoring goals and smashing myths, had some people hailing a revolution. It seemed a tide of change might sweep the globe, pushing old-fashioned notions and gender stereotypes aside while delivering more power to women.

It was also a year when a flurry of appointments in Australia saw women for the first time heading the Reserve Bank (Michelle Bullock), the Australian Competition and Consumer Commission (Gina Cass-Gottlieb), and the Productivity Commission (Danielle Wood), and four women running ASX (Australian Securities Exchange) top 20 organisations: Telstra's Vicki Brady, Macquarie Bank's Shemara Wikramanayake, Woodside Energy's Meg O'Neill and Coles' Leah Weckert. It's progress alright. It speaks volumes about how women are, in fact, ambitious and well qualified enough to take on these roles, given the chance.

But these remarkable women also remain the exception, not the rule. Internationally it seems that welcome wave of post-WWC and *Barbie* euphoria hasn't exactly influenced most power elites as yet. Women are still largely absent from the top table, and the trajectory is so slow it risks sliding in the wrong direction. At the moment, it's definitely still Ken calling the shots.

The decision-makers of today, who are choosing the decision-makers of tomorrow, bear an uncanny resemblance to the decision-makers of the past just about everywhere. That's letting a significant amount of talent go to waste. And it's not as though the current cohort have done a terrific job of running the world either. Glossing over the reality and then claiming we've reached peak gender equity props up this status quo.

As the following chapters make clear, I think there's an urgent need to take a long hard look at what is going on. I've spent many years researching how bias against women leaders operates, and my latest digging shows it hasn't changed – or it has got worse. At the same time, it's clear to me it can be fixed much more quickly than predictions suggest, and better outcomes realised, if some realism and evidence are applied. Painting a rosy but distorted picture of women's status not only lets organisations and the people who run them off the hook, it entrenches scepticism and backlash. It also minimises the sexism women face, and leaves them less likely to speak up about what they face, particularly in senior ranks.

The imbalance that leaves so many white men in powerful roles in Australia has barely shifted in recent years and lags behind some comparable countries. That's not a picture many in the broader community are aware of. A survey in 2023 on gender attitudes of Australians by girls' rights organisation Plan International Australia[1] found most Australians have an overly optimistic view: around 90 per cent believe in the importance of gender equality, but 59 per cent believe that it has mostly or already been achieved. About 58 per cent agree that some jobs are naturally suited to men, indicating gender stereotypes were deeply embedded in Australia.

'One of the key findings for me is the closer you are to the issue, the further away you think gender equality is', Susanne Legena, chief executive of Plan International Australia, told SBS.[2] My sentiments exactly. A closer look at the data I've outlined in this chapter shows we are a long way from equity – and a range of leaders I interviewed agreed.

There's a big gap between perception and reality about women in leadership, says director and Team Global Express CEO Christine Holgate (formerly at Australia Post). Her experience of bullying and harassment played out on the national stage in 2020, after she was attacked in federal parliament for giving a handful of executive's luxury watches as a bonus. Holgate says the sexism she faced as a CEO remains firmly in place despite window dressing about progress, and the statistics are worse than the headlines. Even slow increases of women leading listed companies disguises the lack of change at some of the biggest employers in Australia, which are private companies. Taking that into account, it's been estimated of all the CEOs in the country, less than 5 per cent are women. If you want to be a female CEO of a larger company, your chances are so low you have better odds of winning the lottery, she said.

Even ASX data shows women hold 9 per cent of top 300 Australian-listed company CEO roles, and 18 per cent of top operational and finance roles.[3] In the US, women made up just 10 per cent of CEOs running Fortune 500 companies in 2023.[4] When US researchers looked into the reasons so few made it to the senior ranks, they uncovered a veritable minefield of excuses for the snail's pace. There's always a reason why women are 'never quite right' for leadership roles, they found. Whether it's age, race, parental status or something else, the list was so comprehensive the researchers ended up calling it 'We want what you aren't' discrimination.

A look around the globe shows data on women's progress into top tiers follows a depressing trend. When the World Economic Forum published its 2023 Global Gender Gap Index, it revealed one of the key measurements that continues to lag is the appointment of women into leadership, particularly as the economies in many countries have slowed.[5] Women make up 46 per cent of entry-level roles, but only 25 per cent of executive roles, and for the first time this indicator had dropped backwards to the 2021 level.

This regression perpetuates the 'Drop to the Top' phenomenon—where women's leadership rates decline steadily the further up the chain you go, as journalist Angela Priestley noted.[6] It's continuing, despite the fact women now make up the majority of university enrolments in most countries worldwide. Progress in other arenas, such as education, political representation and health, hasn't surged ahead either: there has been just a 4.1 per cent improvement in progress towards gender equity since the report was first published in 2006.

Perhaps the most compelling international data to confirm how much still needs to be done to change the power equation comes from the UN's Gender Social Norms Index (GSNI). It shows that gender bias is a pervasive problem worldwide. The research measures biases against women, by examining people's attitudes on women's roles along four key dimensions: political, educational, economic and physical integrity.

> The index, covering 85 percent of the global population, reveals that close to 9 out of 10 men and women hold fundamental biases against women. Nearly half the world's people believe that men make better political leaders than women do, and two of five people believe that men make better business executives than women do.[7]

There are major legal impediments for women too. Research released in 2024 by the World Bank found the global gender gap for women in workplaces was far wider than previously thought, and women had fewer than two-thirds the rights of men. This reflects a lack of well implemented equal opportunity laws for pay, childcare and safety. 'No country provides equal opportunity for women – not even the wealthiest economies', the research found.[8]

The resignation of three female heads of government within just a few weeks in early 2023 highlighted how fragile progress has been. New Zealand former prime minister Jacinda Ardern cited the pressure and relentless scrutiny the job entailed; Scotland's former first minister Nicola Sturgeon also pointed to the intensity of the professional and personal coverage she faced; and while Finland's former prime minister Sanna Marin lost an election, she also stood down as chair of the Social Democrats and acknowledged the toll from five years of media attention on her personal life. They were all flag-bearers for women's leadership, and held up as examples of gender change, but it came at a high price. The extra attention they got was hard to face, but can also have a distorting effect, which mistakes a handful of women in the spotlight for widespread progress – and reinforces the idea the problem is pretty much solved.

It turns out less than a third of the UN's 193 member states have ever had a female leader, as noted in several media reports following this trio of departures. Even with a number of female leaders taking office in recent years 'the actual numbers remain incredibly low'.[9] Just 16 UN member states in 2024 have female heads of government, down from 17 in 2022. A study of the 33 biggest multilateral bodies, such as the World Bank and the World Trade Organization, found that of their 382 leaders since 1945, only 47 have been women.[10]

This scenario makes for an increasingly isolated experience for female leaders, according to Iceland's current prime minister, Katrin Jakobsdóttir. 'Numbers have gone down rather than up so it's a lonely place. It's a worrying trend and shows there's nothing given about gender equality ... If we had more women at the table making decisions, we would have less conflict and more focus on the wellbeing of the population.'[11] Her words reflect research showing countries led by women are often happier and healthier than those led by men.

The picture in Australian politics isn't entirely bad news, although men in suits are far from an endangered species. It's been uplifting to see the number of Australian women in elected government increase in some areas. The 2022 federal election resulted in women holding 44.4 per cent of seats across both chambers. There have been 10 women appointed to the Cabinet (43.5 per cent), which is the largest number of women to ever hold positions in that key body.[12]

The shift is welcome and has been a long time coming. In state and territory legislatures, 39 per cent of representatives are women but only two women are leading governments (in Victoria and the Northern Territory). While women are still not as well represented in local government as men, particularly as mayors and CEOs, the number of elected women councillors has increased. But scratch the surface and it's a different picture. In 2021, despite more women working in federal parliament than men, they were overwhelmingly in the lowest paid jobs.[13] Men have traditionally dominated the best paid positions, such as chief of staff and senior adviser.

Federal parliament employees aside, there's better news across the economy, with women increasingly joining the management ranks over recent years, according to the Workplace Gender Equality Agency (WGEA) and Curtin University data. Women held 42.4 per cent of all managerial roles, an increase of 1.7 per cent from 2019 to 2022. But the number of women CEOs had decreased slightly; and 11 per cent of ASX300 chairs and 34 per cent of directors are women, with just 13 per cent of organisations setting targets to change this.[14]

The concentration of men in top jobs also plays out across the economy. Welcome as it is to finally see an increase in elected female politicians and managers, there are a lot of highly paid sectors where women are less likely to be employed at all, much less in leadership. Known as gendered occupational segregation, it hasn't really shifted much in nearly two decades. It remains a real stumbling block to equity because women employees are concentrated in – and then seen as suited to – certain low-paid and low-skilled sectors, such as the caring economy, rather than highly paid areas like finance or resources (the case studies in Chapter 6 show how these demarcations can be successfully tackled).

The trend is getting more pronounced, with fewer women in software programming and construction management, and more in childcare and primary school teaching than three decades ago, according to research by the Committee for the Economic Development of Australia (CEDA). It's a mismatch that limits labour market flexibility, job mobility and productivity, according to Melinda Cilento, CEO of CEDA, and it's mostly due to cultural factors (which include gender stereotypes and bias).[15] On a more positive note, the problem, and its implications for the pay gap, is on the radar of Australia's Fair Work Commission. In 2022, amendments to the Fair Work Act now mean the Commission can take into account work value, and address gender-based undervaluation, to vary award rates.

When it comes to propping up the delusion of progress however, there's one set of data that features all the time: the number of women directors on listed company boards. It's virtually used as a proxy for gender progress but the data warrants closer examination. Despite a decade-long push for change, with women directors reaching about 34 per cent on ASX200 companies, the level drops off significantly across smaller companies and other businesses, with just 20 per cent of boards having gender balance and 22.3 per cent still entirely male.[16]

I was reminded of the deceptive gender data trap during a presentation in 2023 by recruiters Watermark. During the launch of their annual Australian Board Diversity Index, it was pointed out that while there were more women in directorships – and the total number of board seats held by women has increased 80 per cent since 2016 – the overall number of women directors had declined. This is because a cohort of women directors hold multiple roles: just 19 per cent of female directors prepared to serve on boards hold 45 per cent of board seats occupied by women. The increase in the number of women directors over time has been offset by a stubbornly unchanged 'exclusive club' effect, the report stated.[17] The 2024 report showed 91 per cent of directors were from Anglo Celt backgrounds, just 9 per cent of roles were held by directors from non-Anglo backgrounds, only seven roles were filled by Indigenous directors (and held by four directors), and four roles were held by openly LGBTIQ+ directors.

This issue is not confined to Australia. US recruiter Heidrick & Struggles found there was a decrease in 2022 appointments to Fortune 500 boards from under-represented groups: appointments of women were down to 40 per cent from 45 per cent the year before; and racial or ethnic minorities were down from 41 per cent to 34 per cent, which was the result of fewer board positions for black and African Americans (down from 26 per cent to 17 per cent).[18]

The decrease in the diversity of board appointments is partly because the catchment for candidates effectively still comes from a tiny pool of senior executives. By definition, this often excludes marginalised groups unless active interventions are undertaken. While this could be an unfortunate phase following three years of the pandemic, the US study notes that it doesn't reflect a real commitment to diversity and certainly shows how fragile progress has been.

Even in sectors where women make up the majority of employees, the leadership ranks are often dominated by white men. When setting up the Women's Economic Equality Strategy taskforce in 2023, the federal government's discussion paper about the strategy noted, 'Men are typically over-represented in management and leadership roles across most industries. This is particularly the case in mining, construction, utilities and manufacturing. Even in female-dominated industries, men are still more likely to occupy more senior positions.'[19]

The number of women making partner in top Australian law firms (where women routinely outnumber men at graduate intake) has only slowly inched higher to about 33 per cent. Women are still outnumbered in leadership of the Australian public health sector, despite making up three-quarters of the workforce.[20] Women make up 45 per cent of public hospital board chairs, 39 per cent of private hospital CEOs and 38 per cent of state and federal chief medical or health officers.

The gap is even more pronounced for women facing the toxic intersectional barriers of racism and sexism. Those from culturally and racially marginalised groups in Australia face a much tougher set of barriers for fair recognition and reward. Nearly two-thirds of women in this group surveyed by the Diversity Council of Australia said they received fewer opportunities for career advancement than other women, and 85 per cent said they had to work much harder to get recognition.[21]

Making it to the top is difficult in the world of business or government, but the barriers also exist in community and not-for-profit organisations, local government, small business and religious bodies. It says a lot when traditionally conservative religious bodies are calling out the lack of women at the table. In early 2023, the NSW Government announced the composition of its new Religious Communities Advisory Council. A media release from the Multicultural Communities Council of NSW stated that of the 15 members appointed by the Perrottet Liberal government, only two were women.

> Women are now the backbone of religious communities in Australia and yet the Perrottet Government has again deemed them of little significance. Some religious communities have shown more than 60% of attendees are now women and women across many religions are increasingly challenging male dominated structures. This approach by the Government further places NSW women into positions of vulnerability and exploitation.[22]

Women also make up 75 per cent of the NSW social services sector, for example, but again are not as well represented at the top. While smaller organisations have higher levels of women running the show, the picture changes for larger NGOs with revenue above $25 million. In these organisations, women account for 45 per cent of CEOs, 20 per cent of board chairs, 43 per cent of directors and 54 per cent of leadership teams.[23]

Given this backdrop, reports of a post-feminist world look a little overblown. And it seems even those predictions of a boost for women from the COVID-era introduction of new flexibility in many workplaces (although working from home wasn't an option for some) have proved unrealistic (as I examine in Chapter 2). The change in working practices triggered by the pandemic brought about 'only slight progress for women in senior leadership', according to Grant Thornton's 2023 International Business Report (IBR) research into women in medium-sized businesses.[24]

In fact, progress for women has been slow, increasing only half a percentage point to 32.4 per cent in the past year, and only 13 per cent since the research was first undertaken in 2003. At current rates, only 34 per cent of senior leadership positions will be held by women in 2025. The 30 per cent threshold, which had been seen as a 'tipping point' to accelerate action, hasn't quite worked out that way, according to Karitha Ericson, Global Head of Network Capability and Culture.[25] Not exactly time to pop the champagne corks.

This poor report card, and remarkably sluggish pace of change, hasn't stopped the public messaging about gender equity remaining remarkably positive. As well as the attitudes picked up in surveys showing general agreement that it's an important issue, many organisations claim to be equal opportunity workplaces in recruitment ads and other advertising. There are a few reasons why the rosy narrative appears to fall on fertile ground. Perhaps most obviously, there is increasing pressure to provide evidence of progress and avoid well-documented reputational and financial risks from failing to make much headway.

This drives a compliance mentality, which is superficial but surprisingly effective in spinning the line that all is well. When I explained why I was writing this book to some of my peers, they were surprised. They were convinced that while the gender gap wasn't closed, the train had definitely left the station – although maybe they were sick of listening to me. As a business journalist, I'm more than aware of the corporate tap dancing and compliance mentality around these tricky topics. The powerful have a vested interest in holding on to the reins, minimising the problem and maintaining the status quo. There's often more investment in window-dressing to give an impression of change than in efforts to address inequity.

This is known as 'gender washing' and it masks or ignores the evidence of plateauing or deterioration. Gender washing, as academic Rosie Walters points out, is widespread in the business world, where corporations spend multiple millions telling us what they are doing to empower women and girls and make themselves seem more women-friendly than they really are.[26] As an example, pharma group Novartis frequently featured on an annual list of the 100 best companies to work for, and highlighted the progress it had made in employment practices for women. Yet in 2010, the corporation lost the then largest gender pay, promotion and pregnancy discrimination case ever to go to trial in the US.[27]

But not all gender washing looks the same, and 'some can be easier to spot than others', Walters adds. Two varieties are selective disclosure, when corporations publicise improvements in, for example, female boardroom representation, or the gender pay gap, while omitting contradictory or inconvenient information. Another is gender policies that sound positive but do little to move the dial, such as women's mentoring schemes and advice that are focused on fixing women individually rather than tackling biased norms (which I examine in Chapter 5).

Most Australian companies have value statements stressing the commitment to building diverse, equitable and inclusive workplaces. But the rhetoric and reality gap shows up when data or a scandal reveals a different picture. The 2024 publication of individual organisation's gender pay gap showed there is still a long way to go in applying those principles with the lack of women in high paid jobs. A few years ago financial services company AMP faced criticism when it promoted a senior executive (more on this in Chapter 3) who had been fined for sexual harassment, despite public commitments to diversity goals.

But the lack of women in senior roles is increasingly hard to hide. Occasionally all the bluster and glossy pledges can't paper over the reality. This triggers a wave of sheer frustration among those who want to see real change. It emerges every year as International Women's Day (IWD) comes around and there's a flurry of corporate and networking events announced. IWD commemorates the progress of the women's movement and specifically the protests held early last century in New York, London and a range of cities by women without the basic right to vote or an education.

I should mention I've happily presented at many IWD events over the years, partly because it offers a platform to canvas the issues I care about and highlight the need for change. But I'm also aware that IWD can be co-opted into providing an illusion of progress. In early 2023, a survey by the More Voices, More Representation campaign found that nearly 70 per cent of women, trans and non-binary people didn't feel represented at IWD events or in the media. Disability advocate and editor-in-chief of Missing Perspectives Hannah Diviney was part of the campaign. Missing Perspectives covers a range of social impact areas and was founded to challenge the lack of young women in news around the world. For all its flaws, IWD does provide a platform and a chance to make an impact, and earn some income, Diviney told me at the time. But she's also conscious the media treat it like ticking a box while women are fighting the other 364 days of a year for the things that are said on the 8 March. 'It's an excellent opportunity but instead of using it as a springboard to address structural and systemic issues it's used as a distraction,' she said.[28]

In recent years some frustrated women (and men) decided to not just get mad but get even. Clever algorithms have made the contradictions around IWD embarrassingly clear. As various companies used social media to focus on their gender credentials in the UK, a gender pay gap bot picked up classic phrases and then posted organisations' current pay gaps (which can be publicly accessed). Under the banner 'Stop posting platitudes. Start fixing the problem' the posts gathered an enthusiastic following. The founders of this clever intervention, Francesca Lawson and Ali Fensome, said they got tired of IWD messages of empowerment, inspiration and celebration because the sentiments don't reflect the reality we live in. They built the gender pay gap bot to highlight that employers' supportive social media posts are rarely backed up by action.[29] The bot works because 2017 legislation in the UK introduced mandates that employers above a certain size publish their gender pay data. This has been replicated in Australia under amendments to the Workplace Gender Equality legislation, which came into effect just before IWD in 2024. My bet is on a similar bot emerging pretty soon: employers should be on the alert.

Gender washing often causes 'gender fatigue' – an overwhelming feeling that this is a problem that has been over-discussed. It's fuelled by complaints that support for women has gone too far or is unfair, despite the evidence to the contrary. I've been briefed on a number of occasions before a speaking event and told to make sure I don't focus too much on gender or put the men off. It's an odd request given my expertise. But usually it turns out that previous presentations led to complaints that men were being blamed and women were getting too much attention. It's crucial to address other forms of bias, such as ageism, racism, trans- and homophobia, along with sexism. Gender fatigue, however, hasn't come from too much action, but too little, particularly in addressing intersectionality.

The jarring gap between appearance and reality of gender progress isn't confined to blue-chip companies but is also found across sectors such as the start-up space, research bodies and the arts. This can surprise younger women who have grown up in the era of empowerment rhetoric. I was on a panel in mid-2023 with young Indigenous woman, singer and activist Mi-kaisha Masella, who had some insights on where power sits in the music industry, particularly in the production and audio engineering spaces. She later explained to me what she has observed:

I'm realising that there is way, way further to go in achieving representation for women, particularly in the music industry. It's easy to look at the music industry and think, 'Oh, wow, there's plenty of female representation on the Top 100 charts and all my favorite pop stars are women'. But when you look at the people behind the scenes, who call the shots, the people who run the labels, who run the publishing companies, the people who produce the music, who own the publishing and master rights – they are predominantly male. I think right now, stats show that female and non-binary producers, audio engineers and executives make up around 3 per cent of the industry, which is just not good enough.

Unravelling what is going on to explain this increased rhetoric/reality divide across sectors from pop music to politics, I arrived on a late summer morning at the Australian National University campus in Canberra to meet Professor Michelle Ryan, the head of the Global Institute for Women's Leadership. After many years working in the UK, Ryan has had her feet back on Australian soil since 2022, and continues to publish an array of research on gender and leadership. This covers traps employers often fall into while attempting to tackle gender equity – including the tendency for many organisations and employers to be over-optimistic and over-emphasise quantity rather than quality in data, along with relying on fixing women.

Despite some progress, Ryan says, the evidence is pretty clear: women are very much in the minority in many decision-making groups. Yet research consistently shows both men and women overestimate the number of women in these cohorts. 'One of the problems is that many organisations tend to focus on quantity rather than quality when gathering gender data, and this masks the inequity in particular areas', she told me. Gathering information on women and their progress has to be more than broad numbers (quantity), but specifics on where they are employed, and how they are progressing compared to their male peers (quality). This more nuanced information (which potentially can include other areas such as racial background, disability and LGBTIQ+) allows the biased treatment and structures to become apparent, and then helps frame effective responses to it.

In the business world, this is about looking beyond media and marketing efforts, and corporate values, to see not only who is in the top jobs, but who gets the most money – and power. As an example, I noticed that headlines trumpeted the fact that more than 20 per cent of top 50 listed companies were run by women in 2023. But a different picture emerged when the 50 highest paid CEOs in Australia were listed: just two were women.[30] Similarly, as I've mentioned, data showing increased women directors on listed company boards does a lot of heavy lifting in this debate, but much less attention is paid to the low numbers of women chairing boards or in senior executive ranks.

Over-optimism has serious consequences, Ryan's research has found. She said a study of veterinary surgeons found that those who felt sexism was no longer a problem were most likely to pay a female employee less than a man and give her fewer opportunities.[31] Another study found men who overestimated the number of women in medicine were also the least likely to support gender equity programs.[32]

The reason some men in these professions believe gender equality is already solved and then behave in a sexist way could be the result of two factors, the study suggested.

If you don't believe women face discrimination, it could reflect 'a lack of awareness of the subtle ways in which discrimination toward women can manifest itself', the research found.[33] For example, pervasive stereotypes often portray men as more competent, and this can subtly impact how we perceive two individuals, even if they are equally qualified in every way. People who believe these stereotypes may be unlikely to stop and 'check themselves' when showing gender-biased behaviour. There's also the possibility that current social norms, making it unacceptable to be openly sexist, mean these attitudes will only be expressed informally. Saying you believe female vets are treated equally, for example, doesn't automatically mean you reflect that in your actions.

There's another mismatch in the story about women in STEMM (science, technology, engineering, maths, medicine), where the lack of progress has often been identified but misdiagnosed. UNSW ovarian cancer researcher Professor Caroline Ford is a passionate advocate for women in the sector (more on her advocacy efforts in Chapter 7) and says the biology, medicine and the broader science arena has employed women for 50 years in equal numbers. But many recent programs to encourage more women into careers overlook the fact that's not where the obstacles arise, she tells me.

> The problem is that they don't progress, and they
> don't go on to leadership. And it's not a matter of time

and this whole thing about the leaky pipeline – as if there's just this passive removal of women – but they are forced out because the system is not designed for them, and they're not welcome. I think this narrative that women are choosing to leave is so wrong, because there's not a system that's actually built for them or supporting them and making them feel included.
To be brutally honest, I think a lot of the money has been wasted, and it was seen as an easy win (by government) to put money into Women in STEMM programs. Because it's a popular thing that could show that they've done something about, but I don't think it changes the systems at all.

Programs to increase gender balance in science, such as Athena Swan, which was set up in the UK, have had more success Ford adds, giving accreditation to universities and medical research institutes that show gender progress through reporting. The example of astronomy research centre Astro3D in Chapter 6 shows an evidence-based strategy can deliver results quite quickly. But 'just shoving more women into a broken system is ultimately not going to be to anyone's benefit', Ford says.

This observation on STEMM programs for women, and the research on vets, show that 'it's important to reveal the actual data on women, but also examine how it's perceived,' Ryan says. If there's a belief that more change has been made or the problem is women themselves, there can well be an unintended result that stymies diversity programs. 'We need to be realistic about where we are, and how much there is still to do,' she adds. When it comes to organisational over-optimism, there was often a strong compliance mentality at play, particularly when there are programs with lists of actions to complete, she tells me.

> So it becomes this sort of tick box exercise. And then people say 'I've ticked the box. I don't have to do anything anymore'. I think that is part of the problem. So whether it's through fatigue, or whether it's because of a 'Oh, yeah, we've done that'. Or some senior person says, 'I'm sure that someone in HR has got that covered' or 'I've seen something in the report that said that we're dealing with it', then it's no longer their problem. And that's partly why you've got to embed it, to make sure that it's everyone's problem, not just someone in HR that's ticking the boxes that allows you to move on.

Collecting and applying nuanced data on gender equity counters another damaging trend. It challenges the belief that women have just about the same opportunities and support as men these days. So if they run into any barriers, it's not to do with gender and it is up to them to sort out the problems. These beliefs can affect managers and anyone handling diversity programs, which results in the fixing approach (which I examined in detail in my book *Stop fixing women*).

Instead of looking at the bias woven through rules and norms, the blame is shunted onto women's shoulders and they are told to toughen up or behave more like men. As Ryan explains, this trend has also been fanned by the era of corporate empowerment – including 'lean in' – the term coined by former Facebook executive Sheryl Sandberg, who wrote a book of the same name that encouraged women to modify their behavior and take the lead in addressing sexism. 'It gives women the illusion that they can take control. That wave of thinking held out the idea that individual women can do it, and if it doesn't work, then you haven't "leaned in" enough,' Ryan tells me.

Even in areas receiving much needed attention, such as workplace sexual harassment and bullying, the belief the problem has been identified and taken seriously is superficial at best. In 2023 Deloitte researchers found that only 59 per cent of women who said they were harassed reported the incidents to their employer, down from 66 per cent in the prior year's survey.[34] The decline in reporting is not due to decreasing harassment.

> Experts across the legal, academic and HR fields say the reasons for the decrease in reporting is likely the result of a combination of factors: from fear of retaliation, to a sense that the behaviour or actions might just not be serious enough to warrant a report.
>
> But the experts also agree not reporting harassment, or not creating the type of work environment in which women feel comfortable reporting problematic behaviour, will only serve to make the problem worse. If the economic landscape grows even more uncertain, then women might find themselves in a double bind: feeling compelled to stay quiet about inappropriate behaviour in the workplace, while also worrying about their job security and career progression.[35]

The frustration of women over this failure to make headway on their safety at work is bubbling away and occasionally erupting – not only on IWD. The allegations made by young political staffer Brittany Higgins in 2021, who alleged she was raped in Parliament House, triggered a wave of activism and political upheaval around Australia. The Sex Discrimination Commissioner at the time, Kate Jenkins, ran the Respect@Work inquiry and eventually made comprehensive recommendations for an overhaul of rules and protocols, which were legislated in full. One of the newer obligations is an onus on employers to provide a safe working environment for all employees, which took effect from late 2023, and increases pressure for meaningful action.

This will put pressure on employers to use an evidence-based approach to close the gap between lip service and outcomes for safer workplaces, with clear data, programs and accountability for progress. This is more than doable for many medium-to-larger organisations. Most Australian employers already have obligations to report on various gender equity measures to WGEA, which covers 11 000 Australian employers.

That said, consistently monitoring DEI (diversity, equity and inclusion) outcomes hasn't been top of the list for many organisations to date. Bianca Hartge-Hazelman is founder of gender equality monitor the Financy Women's Index, and equality tech platform IMPACTER, and a former business journalist. She says organisations that want to be compliant with where things are going with gender reporting also have an obligation to capture and analyse accurate data. The link to financial outcomes from taking action also has to be clearly established, she adds, and this motivated her to develop IMPACTER to capture this information.

> We're not at a tipping point on social impact where organisations say this is absolutely the critical thing to do. It's unfortunate and dangerous because from a regulatory perspective, Australian businesses need to be taking proactive steps not just to support greater gender equality and diversity but to help eliminate discrimination and harassment in the workplace. The penalties for non-compliance are significant. At the same time, there is so much research out there that shows companies which are more inclusive do actually perform better and this is where our IMPACTER tech is such a timely and important tool because we provide a centralised measurement tool that helps business leaders and HR managers report to regulators.

Like Hartge-Hazelman, my years as a business journalist have left me well aware of the temptation for employers to gloss over the slow progress and barriers, then sweep the problem under the carpet along with the chance to find viable interventions. But the serious financial and risk repercussions from sticking with business-as-usual are increasing, while the data mounts on the significant benefits from better gender balance, not just at the top but throughout organisations.

Debunking the progress narrative is clearly about reining in the hubris and delivering on programs for women at every level. That means investing where it counts: less mentoring, remedial workshops and unconscious bias training; and more gender pay gap audits, transparency of progression criteria and feedback, and vetting for sexism/bias in recruitment and performance management. This also helps counter the informal but influential idea that supporting women is part of political correctness gone awry.

Oddly enough, over-optimism actually distracts from the reasons to be optimistic, particularly when women get a chance to join the decision-making table. Robust academic, peer-reviewed research linking more women in leadership with improved outcomes is on the increase. It's about return on investment, and bottom-line impact, plus better innovation, governance and less risk exposure, according to a list of compelling international studies compiled by Tomas Chamorro-Premuzic, a professor of business psychology at University College London. Establishing this link is not about putting pressure on women to improve results or show they have 'superior' skills, but as he points out, accessing a broader set of expertise from a cohort that is generally better educated: 'Unlocking gender diversity is a serious business opportunity at all levels'.[36] If there were more attention paid to this solid evidence rather than expensive gender washing to disguise inertia, we'd all be a lot better off.

The lack of women in decision-making has often been disguised by platitudes or complacency, but there's some critical issues at stake, says University of Technology Sydney law academic Ramona Vijeyarasa. Her work on women leading governments, particularly in South-East Asia, revealed that the impact of women leaders on gender outcomes isn't automatically positive and varies across countries. There are, though, some possible areas of difference: women leaders were more likely than men to appoint women to senior roles, enact gender equality laws and have a role model effect.[37] Yet few people were mapping the low numbers of women holding these roles, and the sheer lack of progress for women decision-makers in government and other sectors. That matters a lot to all of us, she told me in an interview, and yet this is an era where we've achieved so little, which makes her wonder why no one's speaking about that.

> In no other context, would women accept 15 per cent representation and be OK with that. And so even now, we're sort of hitting 30 per cent women in some spaces, on some boards or in senior leadership or in law firm partnerships. And we're not okay with that: at least I'm not okay with that. So why are we okay with 15 per cent of global leadership?

> I think the ramifications are very significant beyond the representational factor. Women are not present in global decision making. That's fundamental in shaping policy decisions and what's happening over in the G20 is going to shape Europe's leadership on global matters … So if women aren't in those decision-making tables, we are not playing a part in shaping the way the world is and deciding how we want the world to look in the future.

What women are asking for is a fundamental say in their own futures. But as Vijeyarasa explained to me, we also need to be conscious of the fact that what we're asking for is more power. That means taking power from those who have it, so of course, there's going to be backlash. You can't tackle that, as we will see in Chapter 3, if you exaggerate progress towards gender equity – or deny the problem actually exists.

The evidence mapped out here shows that rumours about the death of gender inequity are exaggerated, and over-optimism is hindering, not helping, much-needed interventions. The data shows women are failing to make inroads to top jobs regardless of the sector, despite increasing numbers at management level. Yet many Australians still believe that reaching gender equity is just a matter of time. This dangerous mismatch is occurring just as reporting regimes are putting pressure on employers to make sure they are accountable for concrete action.

The progress narrative has a personal effect on women too, because it's the latest form of benevolent sexism. As it becomes more difficult to maintain arguments that women lack skills and ability for top jobs, defenders of the status quo have a new tactic. They are patronisingly assuring women that momentum towards equity is in hand and they mustn't worry – or speak up. It's another reason for a much-needed reality check and a focus on genuine progress instead of turning a blind eye to the corrosive bias women face.

Chapter 2

Breaking down
the bias barriers

If you ever need a masterclass in decision-making, watch parents of young children negotiating their day. Making constant risk assessments, and sometimes life-saving choices, is part of the job description. The bulk of child rearing and snap decisions when speedy toddlers are reaching for a cup of hot coffee is still mostly women's work. But despite the Mother's Day rhetoric about it being the most important job in the world, it's expected, under-valued and even stigmatised.

On the other hand, there's certainly been some well overdue good news for mothers in Australia over the past few years. The introduction and welcome changes in the scope of paid parental leave (PPL), through legislation and work-place policies, have been a game changer – and have shifted norms, too. Not too long ago, Australia was one of a handful of countries without PPL, with critics claiming it would send us broke. The opposite happened: introducing 18 weeks of paid leave for primary carers at the minimum wage in 2011 has boosted the economy. In 2023, Impact Economics and Policy found that since then, PPL has resulted in 74 245 more women with children aged under five participating in employment, building tenure and skills, and adding $8.5 billion to GDP in 2021–22.[1]

There's now an opportunity to build on this investment and make the most of women's increased workforce participation. PPL was hard fought for, and a crucial step towards closing the gender gap, but it's a start, not an end in itself. A compliance mentality means employers often rely on parenting leave provisions to do the heavy lifting when it comes to tackling gender inequity. But it can't be expected to help overthrow structural sexism and other progression barriers that block women's paths into seniority, whether they have kids or not. No babies doesn't automatically mean no bias.

With the progress narrative and over-optimism on the increase, addressing basic gender bias is a key step in getting women into leadership. But it has slipped down the agenda. It's time to refocus on the growing menu of evidence about how these corrosive beliefs operate, as I'll examine later. While you can't legislate to fix every bias barrier, there are plenty of ways to change rules and practices (more details are outlined in Chapters 5 and 6) once the barriers are identified. That's when attitudes shift.

Watching how PPL has started to alter ideas about who takes time off for the baby is a case in point. When I began reporting on motherhood penalties in paid work in the 1990s, maternity leave (as it was known) was still regarded as a nuisance and mums were expected to be grateful to hang on to their jobs. If they thought about it at all, the bosses I interviewed had some pretty unreconstructed views (putting it politely).

A CEO of a large financial services company once told me the reason he had so few senior women employees was not a lack of PPL, flexibility or motherhood bias when they came back to work. It was the wonderful weather in Sydney, which made it so much nicer to spend time outside than in an office, he said. An academic from a prestigious US university I interviewed about leadership once told me women on parenting leave should really use the time to do an MBA. I politely asked if he had children? No, he did not.

This kind of delusional thinking sounds pretty ridiculous now. But I'm not sure whether there's a more genuine understanding of what happens after PPL: women's double shift of paid and unpaid work, and the complex impact it has on job tenure, pay and progression. There's so much more to be done to support and include mothers (and dads) who return to their jobs and are expected to fit into jobs structured for a full-time male breadwinner. Men are still far less likely to use PPL, making up 14 per cent of all those who take paid primary carer parental leave.[2]

The 'mummy track' is where prospects and pay packets shrivel. It's part of maternity discrimination, which I was covering decades ago and, unfortunately, continues. Even privileged women quickly find out how pregnancy and blatant sexism go hand in hand: a woman told me how her male bosses in a professional organisation chuckled about her being 'up the duff' and highly emotional – right in front of her.

While it's great to make PPL more generous, it's not so great to then penalise mothers for taking that leave. In fact there's evidence those motherhood skills are actually great ingredients for all kinds of leadership, according to Sally McNamara from RMIT.[3] The skills identified include adaptability; collaboration; communication; creativity; emotional awareness and regulation; empathy; humility; inclusion; innovation; problem solving; resilience; self-awareness and more. Sometimes patience and regulating emotions come in very handy at work. A friend who is a financial services manager says her job often feels like running a creche for demanding adults.

Meanwhile, parenting demands haven't exactly eased off as women have increasingly entered paid workplaces. Some would say they have ratcheted up, with dreaded 'helicopter' or 'tiger' parents stigmatised for their over-weening style. But no matter the intensity of the role, the lion's share of child caring is still seen as women's work, regardless of their earning status. Even when women are primary breadwinners, they do the larger share of caring and housework, according to a number of studies.[4] Quite often, this division of labour allows their partner to maintain the long-hours schedule of an 'ideal worker'.

This unpaid-work stalemate extends into a new version of the glass ceiling: not only is the number of hours you work critical to your progression, but where you do your job – in the workplace or working from home (WFH). Jobs that demand long hours (usually held by men and well paid) are out of the question for many women with caring roles and means they confront a 'glass-hours ceiling', according to ANU researchers. This can also impact men who do more of the caring as they find their time spent on paid work also lowers.[5]

Although the pandemic had a major impact on flexible work, it didn't quite end up the way many predicted. For women who could incorporate remote work, and had added supervising their kids' education to their daily unpaid workload, there was a welcome recognition that it was viable. But that didn't last. Since the lockdowns ended, there have been increasing calls to limit WFH and get back to the workplace, with threats of penalties for non-compliance. As journalist Sean Kelly pointed out, 'rather than building on the potential gains for women from the pandemic, some businesses are reducing them. But it is far worse than that: they are taking those gains and actively turning them against women, making them another barrier to success'.[6]

Similarly there have been dire warnings that WFH means losing out on progression because of not being seen at the coalface or privy to corridor chats (known as proximity bias). I believe it's open to debate if women were really involved in most of these chats anyway, and from what I've heard, many found the positives of WFH far outweighed the unlikely prospect of promotion.

The recent moves to encourage men to take parental leave, and hopefully more flexibility, could help efforts to start shifting these tenacious job and care expectations. But it will not happen smoothly. At the moment, it turns out the penalties faced by women taking parental leave are being confronted by men who take up the option, too. Researchers at Melbourne University found more than half of male caregivers, 55 per cent, believe they are treated unfairly at work and nearly one-third, 31 per cent, believe they lost their jobs because of caregiving, compared with 22 per cent of working mothers.[7]

The stigma for men taking parental leave can be a real blocker. Construction company Laing O'Rourke has offered men generous paid parenting leave since 2012, but it's only started to be more regularly used since 2020, Annabel Crookes, Director – Legal, Risk & Delivery at the company, told me. 'It's an example that shows how long it can take for the stigmatising of cultural change to diminish', she says.

There's another tricky reality about the trade-off between short-term, practical flexibility that helps carers, and long-term shifts in gender roles. Flexible workplace policies designed to improve gender gaps might actually make things worse for women if these options aren't normalised, and bias isn't reduced. Policies that make it easier to transition to a part-time job or take leave may actually be weakening women's position in the labour market and their lifetime earnings potential, therefore widening gender gaps in pay, according to two researchers from Melbourne University, Leah Ruppanner and Jordy Meeks.[8] They point out that the career penalty for women in the current system is felt long beyond the period of maternity leave.

Programs to help women return to work after PPL haven't exactly spread like wildfire either, despite the rhetoric. Sam Turner, a former DEI (diversity, equity, and inclusion) executive at Westpac and Microsoft, and now Chief People Officer at law firm Allens, says she's yet to see a company deliver return from parental leave programs well, regardless of what is reported. I think paying more attention to smoothing the transition back from PPL would not only address bias but help women a lot more than mentoring schemes, empowerment rhetoric or tips on how to turbo-charge your self-confidence.

Ideally, both the expectations of high-status jobs and the value of caring need an overhaul to change these attitudes. Just don't hold your breath. There hasn't been much shift in the realities around women and flexibility, Colleen Ammerman, director of the Race, Gender & Equity Initiative at Harvard Business School (and co-author of *Glass Half Broken* with Boris Groysberg) told me. While hybrid models (combining some days in the workplace with WFH) have been widespread, there haven't been many formal shifts in employer policies to address the barriers faced by women, as Ammerman notes.

> I don't know that they're [employers] really thinking about this question of how to avoid the flexibility stigma and its consequences. I think they feel forced to be more flexible, but they're not necessarily being thoughtful about the framing and the messaging around flex work and remote work. And then there's the issue of, you're a manager and you've got some people who are hybrid or remote and some are more in person – how are you then perceiving their competence and their performance?

Family-friendly policies can often push women off the leadership track, Ammerman and Groysberg found, and 'reinforced notions that they couldn't handle the demands of higher-level roles. When workplaces funnel women into lower-status, less rewarding jobs out of a well-meaning desire to "support" their careers, they further entrench the expectation that women's primary role is outside of the office'.[9] In turn, the division of labour in many homes reinforces the norm that a man is the priority breadwinner. These beliefs were the same for Gen X: younger women's 'lowered expectations for egalitarian caregiving are a reminder that progress toward gender equality is stalled at home, not just at work, in ways that reinforce women's disadvantage in both domains'. Work–family conflict as the core explanation for the lack of women in leadership can actually distract from barriers such as biased behaviours and attitudes, and as a result less time is then spent addressing discrimination, they suggest.[10]

Even if they're not mothers, women are judged against expectations of stereotypical feminine skills that are synonymous with caring – collegiate, empathetic, consultative – not with being the boss. It starts from childhood when girls in particular are told to play nicely, share their toys and not be bossy. Actor America Ferrera, who appeared in the *Barbie* movie, was asked what the difference was between being bossy and being a boss? Being a woman, she replied.

It's no wonder that women, regardless of their parenting status, feel pressure to meet these standards – and face howls of criticism if they don't somehow comply. Julia Gillard's experience shows that women who don't have children also face bias because they haven't followed the script. Many of us remember the palaver about an empty fruit bowl in a photograph of Gillard at home a few years before she became prime minister. It was used to reinforce her as a cold, heartless and, as one male politician infamously claimed, 'deliberately barren' woman. All that from the lack of a few bananas.

There's little evidence that more of this group of women have been able to ascend into authority or decision-making ranks, leaving their reproducing sisters in their wake. In fact, a significant number of the small cohort of women CEOs and government leaders globally have children.

Researchers examining the gender-based attitudes faced by women leaders in the US found that whatever their parental status, it was a major point of criticism.

> Women can't win whether they have kids or not: One single, divorced lawyer and mother of pre-schoolers says she was passed up for career opportunities 'due to a perception by my male bosses that I cannot or should not handle [larger matters].' Meanwhile, a child-free physician was expected to work harder and accomplish more than other female colleagues with child-care responsibilities, according to the study.[11]

Far too often this double bind is either ignored or blamed on women's 'choices'. But choice is about viable options. Women continue to face backlash and judgement in workplaces and the community when they don't comply with binary social norms of being a 'good mother' or a serious worker.

Both babies and bias are acting as brakes on women's progress up the ranks, the Victorian Gender Equality Commissioner, Dr Niki Vincent told me. Her work involves implementing the gender equality legislation introduced in Victoria in 2020, which requires the public sector to collect data, report on and address gender equity. While there is only one set of data so far, some broader trends are apparent, Vincent explained to me in an interview.

> We still have a very big gap between the number of women in each organisation and the number of women in leadership and in the public service. That's a 25 per cent gap. The same in local government and

in broader organisations as well, it's a 20 per cent gap. So the public service, for all of its good work, has the biggest gap alongside of local government. I feel like we can only get so far with everything that we're doing without adjusting the men looking after the kids factor. Because at some point, women cannot do any more, even if they're in a senior leadership role which is a job share, and they've got flexibility. But they still have another job to do when they get home. So often, I see women completely exhausted and stressed out in those jobs.

It would also help enormously to have a much wider range of options in how workplaces operate and jobs are designed (more on this in Chapter 6) to reflect the demands faced by many women – and some men. Nobel Prize–winning economist Claudia Goldin has studied these issues for decades and points out that high-paying jobs come with an expectation of availability, are time greedy, and are dominated by men who have wives or partners at home to prop up their careers.[12] Job sharing or having a roster of colleagues who can substitute for each other can make a big difference, Goldin points out. Managerial innovation to allow this can make jobs more mother-friendly: 'The firm, given the incentives, can always find a way to have good substitutes'.

Offering flexibility and then penalising those taking it doesn't make much sense. And neither does spending money on PPL then treating women unfairly when they return to work. In fact, the main reasons women leave their jobs is not flexibility but how they are treated and paid once they get back to the workplace. A survey of thousands of US academics revealed the number-one reason that women leave was poor 'workplace climate', including discrimination, dysfunctional leadership, and a feeling of not fitting in.[13] Research in Australia found that 60 per cent of mothers returning to work after parental leave believe their opinions are often ignored, they feel excluded, and they are given unmanageable workloads.[14]

Flexibility is a no-brainer for women in employment and helps with tenure. But as long as it comes with a stigma, it can't challenge the long-hours mentality that defines senior jobs. A scant 7 per cent of Australian management jobs are part-time, for example, with the number dropping the more senior the role.[15] Just 5 per cent of senior management and 3 per cent of CEOs work part-time. Focusing on viable ways of redesigning top roles would make a big difference to women and men.

Motherhood stereotypes are part of a thicker layer of gender bias that stymies women, regardless of their parenting status. I've written about some of this insidious sexism over the years but as I reviewed the latest data, it became clear it's still part and parcel of women's experiences at work. The data doesn't just corroborate what is happening but also how employers can deal with it. Addressing bias hinges on recognising these inaccurate but widespread beliefs about women's capacity for decision-making and authority, ageism, lookism, the toxic effects of intersectionality, the glass cliff – and our tolerance of alpha male over-confidence and hubris.

Who wears the pants?

There's nothing imaginary or benign about the negative way female leaders are still perceived. As I've noted, the pandemic clearly didn't help with a return to traditional ideas of who makes a better leader, according to analysis of an international survey that found trust in women leaders has fallen.[16] More men than women employees reported a lack of trust in female executives, according to 2022/23 data from The Reykjavik Index for Leadership, a survey comparing men's and women's suitability for positions of power. Worryingly, the Index also showed that young people hold more prejudice against women's suitability for leadership than their parents.

The decline in trust was possibly a reaction to the perception that female leaders were disruptive to the 'business as usual' narrative. That presumably means assertive blokes like former Qantas CEO Alan Joyce, and Tesla's Elon Musk, who have erratic track records, are tolerated more than the few women in charge. Some of this lack of trust also comes from gendered assumptions about women's decision-making capacity – lack of decisiveness, poor ability under pressure and risk aversion. These beliefs are mostly inaccurate, exaggerated or depend on context, but never let the facts get in the way of a widely believed story.

The bias and scepticism about women's capacity to handle power also runs through social norms. Popular culture is full of lame jokes and images of bossy housewives driving the menfolk crazy with strategising, over-organising, budgeting and detailed decision-making. It's rare to see any acknowledgment that these are the exact skills needed to be an effective manager.

Even in relationships and the home, the sphere seen as most suited to women, traditional ideas of who is really 'the boss' still exist in some households. A series of embarrassing revelations about former NSW premier Gladys Berejiklian and her then boyfriend, former MP Daryl Maguire, were a sharp reminder of this. In a recorded conversation, Maguire tells his partner that even though she is the premier of the state, he is still the boss.

As columnist Jenna Price commented, deciding who the best decision-maker is should really depend on the decision. But she also noted that research shows:

> One in three men agree that 'women prefer a man to be in charge of the relationship' compared with only one in five women. Twice as many men (21 per cent, or one in five) agree that 'men should take control in relationships and be the head of the household', as compared with one in 10 women. …

> Is it about men earning more? Thinking that because they earn the big bucks, they get to take charge? And what would happen if women started charging out for the mental load? For the cognitive work they do in keeping relationships and connections alive? Money's good but love matters more.[17]

These assumptions about who is the boss in relationships and families are far from harmless. They need to be challenged, as domestic violence expert and Women's Community Shelters NSW CEO Annabelle Daniel tells me over a coffee. Those traditional beliefs are clearly at odds with the reality of many women's lives where they are often making decisions about the family or in the workplace, but their input is less valued or recognised. Not only are most women just as experienced in making decisions under stress, men are also vulnerable to irrational and emotional decision lapses, she explained to me.

> What I always find interesting in that space, too,
> is a lot of lawyers and court professionals talk
> about the quality of the decisions that judges make
> during the day. You're far better off getting a court
> slot in the morning or when they've just had lunch.
> And you think, well, if you were the best possible
> decision-maker, those anomalies would have been
> addressed by now. So-called logical decision-
> making actually revolves around how hungry
> we are, or whether we are tired, and how much
> bandwidth we actually have left.

Research on this is quite compelling. It shows that when judges (many of whom are men) are weary and hungry, they tend towards a harsher option, such as denying parole.[18] It's unsurprisingly been tagged the 'hungry judge syndrome'. Apparently, powerful men can also become tired and emotional.

Traditional ideas about who is entitled to make the decisions has serious repercussions in the domestic violence sphere, Daniel pointed out. A typical pattern of abuse in families involves deliberately removing and belittling women's capacity to have a say. The dynamics in many work-places are different, of course, but there are some similar stifling effects on women from having their authority and input ignored or belittled.

Education on masculine norms and their effect is being used to tackle some of these beliefs. The 2023 pilot study of the Modelling Respect and Equality Schools program (MoRE), by Jesuit Social Services and the Men's Project, was conducted in 58 Victorian schools. The education program changed attitudes: 72 per cent of school staff found it deepened their understanding of the link between supporting healthier masculinities and preventing violence against women; two out of three MoRE Champions intended to make change in their school culture and environment.[19] In business, there's growing demand for education, too. Queensland University of Technology Professor Michael Flood, an expert in gender norms, often gets asked by large companies to speak to audiences of men and women about the benefits of abandoning rigid gender stereotypes.

Intersectionality penalties

The combination of sexism and racism can lead to particularly toxic outcomes for women in leadership or those with aspirations for authority. Asian Australian women face a complex array of gender and cultural assumptions, according to DEI expert Julie Chai, who founded the Asian Leadership Project to address this 'bamboo ceiling' (more on this in Chapter 6). She asked a number of the high-achieving professional women in her network about what they faced in their jobs with well-known Australian employers.

Several said bias meant they were seen as not assertive enough to speak up or to have a voice at the table, were too agreeable, and therefore take longer to make decisions or were not seen as able to make tough calls. The flip side of being stereotypically labelled as quiet and 'good workers' was being perceived as less decisive and capable leaders. Some women reported being pigeonholed as passive compliant, not movers and shakers, because they are less curious and accept things as presented to them. They're seen as less likely to ask a lot of questions or challenge authority, and problem-solve on their own instead of asking for help.

Women from a range of backgrounds are far less likely to feel included in many workplaces, says Allens' Sam Turner, who is an advocate for the LGBTIQ+ community. There's a lot of lip service that goes into LGBTIQ+ inclusion but she overwhelmingly sees women in the workplace who are closeted, and feel like they don't have as much career progression. The firm's inclusion score is 80 per cent but for LGBTIQ+ women, that drops to 50 per cent, she pointed out. That 30 per cent difference in how included they feel would be even greater for queer people of colour, or any other intersection. But it makes quite a difference if there are visible allies tackling bias, as Turner explained to me.

> This still comes down to critical mass, and certainly my experience when I was in banking, I was lucky to be the only woman in the room, or maybe two other women around the table on my leadership team. And so why on earth would I then 'other' myself even more, I then become the lesbian or the Korean woman or the non-binary person? I think it's now different for me as a very senior person who's very out, you've just got to know that I'm queer. But I think having

that role model now, in quite a conservative firm, it is game changing for the LGBTIQ+ community.

The effect of role models, networks and support can make a difference to negative social experiences in quite profound ways. Dealing with environments where there is less inclusion and fewer role models can actually change the brain in dramatic ways, including in terms of inhibition, says Pro-fessor Emeritus of Cognitive Neuroimaging at Aston University, Gina Rippon. People tend to withdraw from situations if they feel they're likely to encounter a negative experience and these findings have implications for employers.

> People who are trying to look at diversity and inclusion initiatives within organizations really need to be aware that the diversity aspect isn't enough, it's the inclusion aspect, which is really important, because our brains are wired to make us social. So if we're feeling that we're approaching an organization where we're not going to be included, we're not going to be rewarded, we may be constantly bombarded with what might be called banter about what people like you can and can't do, then it's much more likely that these people withdraw from that situation, they will not choose it.[20]

Risky behaviour

The perception that all women, regardless of context, naturally lack an appetite for risk is an irritatingly tenacious example of sexism. A more nuanced understanding of where this assumption comes from, and the role of defining risk and context, is showing a rather different picture, however. Under pressure, studies show men tend to take more risky and women less risky decisions, which also suggests having a mix of gender at the table is likely to produce the best decisions.[21]

A growing body of research on women and board decision-making has also busted a few myths about the way these dynamics work. 'Women serving on boards are willing to ask in-depth questions and engage with the issues reflecting both autonomy and rationality, attributes stereotypically not attributed to women in the workplace', according to strategic management academics Professor Margarethe Wiersema, University of California, and Professor Marie Louise Mors, Copenhagen Business School.[22]

While theories of group behaviour predict that female directors would seek to belong to the elite club of the board, and thus not stand out or deviate from board norms, these findings show that they appear to be less worried about how they are perceived and less likely to adhere to board norms. That sounds potentially like quite risky behaviour, if you think about it.

And just how much of this behaviour is intrinsic? If women are cautious it's probably due to their relatively disempowered status rather than to biology – many women will think twice before risking what little they have, according to researchers from business school INSEAD.[23] While a belief that women have an allergy to risk-taking is still widespread in the venture capital area, the reality was more complicated than initially believed, they found.

Traditionally defined risk-taking behaviours are biased towards men, while risk-taking behaviours engaged by women were less defined or studied. It seems to me that the nature of the topic being discussed also makes quite a difference – are financial or venture capital decisions more likely to be labelled risky than tricky moral or ethical decisions?

The biggest risk for female entrepreneurs is probably running up against a mansplaining tech know-it-all who is in denial about sexism. A few years ago I was on a panel discussing female entrepreneurs and a well-known male tech personality scoffed at the notion that bias or sexism played any part in venture capital decisions. 'We are gender-blind and only interested in good ideas, no matter where they come from', he claimed.

A few of the speakers pointed out that bias definitely inhibits women who still run into major barriers in raising capital and getting their ideas taken seriously. According to a women's start-up network, Scale Investors, only 4 per cent of start-up funding between 2018 and 2021 went to all-women teams, and around 3 per cent of venture capital goes to women-led businesses.[24] These arguments, however, didn't convince the tech identity, who couldn't accept that bias had any role in his finely tuned decisions.

Financial acumen

Tackling the gender bias around risk and decision-making is critical because it unlocks a very different picture about basic aptitude and competency for leadership. I've also written a lot about the belief that women can't handle money, particularly the strongly recycled idea that women aren't interested in or struggle to become financially literate. I once heard a leading financial executive explain that far fewer women than men can define compound interest or inflation – which is one way of assessing knowledge.

But looked at in another way, women have lots of experience to draw on. Many run household budgets and can work out a 25 per cent discount when shopping at the drop of a hat. The number of women enrolling in management or commerce degrees is about 47 per cent,[25] and women make up the fastest growing cohort of Australian sharemarket investors. This is helping to skewer the idea they don't have the capacity to make decisions and assess risk.[26]

Women may, however, find their skills are questioned far more often than their male peers. I spoke to advocate and trans woman Sally Goldner, a former accountant, who explained what she'd experienced before and after transitioning:

> You start realising just how much, when you don't
> have the privilege, the sort of things that change.
> So my original line of work, for example, was
> accounting. Every year all of us would come in, and,
> you know, as a male, they just look at everything I've
> done and green tick, green tick, green tick. Whereas
> once I was a woman, suddenly they'd come in and
> go, 'Well, you've changed that so you know, that's
> that debit and net credit', and be very patronising and
> mansplaining and misogynist. And it's like, 'Hey,
> look at how you're talking to me?'

A new story is slowly emerging about women's appetite for and skills in finance, with both personal security and professional implications. Skewering this gender bias can help motivate women to pursue finance careers, some of the best paying and most powerful jobs. A few smart women have spotted a gap in the market, and set up programs to help younger women start investing and take control of their finances, which are making an impact, too.

Mariam Mohammed, founder of website Money Girl with Melissa Ma, decided to set up the personal finance education platform in 2019. It particularly targets young women of colour and migrants, because Mohammed realised there was very little in the market for women like her. 'All I had was white finance bros. I wanted a format that was easy and engaging and evidence based, covering tax and superannuation to investing', she told me. Since then more than 400 young women have completed their online courses and the online community has grown to around 2000. One of the most popular topics is share investing, particularly in tech businesses and start-ups, even with women just beginning their careers. 'They understand the importance of wealth management not just security', she says. 'They might start with micro-investing of $500. It's very exciting in fin tech to see how accessible investing is becoming.'[27]

Age before beauty

If they're not running into bias about their aptitude, skills and appetite for finance, risk and decision-making, women have long been up against stringent appearance and age standards. While men also face some of these expectations, it's women who bear the brunt of the criticism, particularly in leadership where the parameters of 'acceptable' age and looks are narrow, and fraught (more on this in Chapter 5). This is particularly the case on social media. Women who object to the finger wagging about their wrinkles or outfits are often told they are over-reacting (the irony), or to suck it up.

Sometimes older women find that, despite being ignored more than when they were younger, their experience and a lack of inhibition can be quite liberating (I may be speaking from experience). But ageism isn't confined to older women: no matter what stage of life, women can run into impediments. It can be used to justify bias and discrimination against women; and there is no right age for professional women, according to researchers who surveyed female leaders in four US sectors (higher education, faith-based nonprofits, law and health care).

> We discovered that many women suffered from this
> 'never right' age bias. Conceptions of young, middle
> and old age are often based on perceptions and vary
> between workplaces and contexts ... As women age,
> they are often not seen as valuable or relevant in the
> way that male counterparts are.[28]

Whatever their age, many of the women surveyed found it was used as an excuse to not take them seriously, discount their opinions or not promote them. The pressure to look young and attractive, or 'lookism', also came through in the ageism data. The child-bearing stage of life is clearly not the only inhibitor for women, with bias facing younger, middle-aged and, of course, older women.

Younger women were routinely called pet names or even patted on the head. They were also mistaken for students or support staff, something that was particularly prevalent for non-white women especially those with Asian heritage. The respondents were more likely to face a 'credibility deficit' and have their expertise questioned than male peers. But as the researchers note, you can't fix a problem unless it's recognised. Organisations need to include training to ensure that age and appearance bias doesn't become a 'hidden metric' for recruitment and promotion, and rather than focusing on age when hiring or promoting, turn attention to each woman's skills.

Credibility gaps and glass cushions

In professional spheres, women often have to face far more scrutiny and scepticism about their work and achievements. Even highly experienced women face scepticism and mansplaining, with female US Supreme Court judges interrupted four times more often than their male peers, according to UK author Mary Ann Sieghart.[29] Julia Gillard reported running into benign sexism as prime minister, with an assumption by some men that the correct relationship with the head of government was almost 'nice uncle to favourite niece'.[30]

A more toxic example was uncovered when senior economists Alicia Sasser Modestino and Justin Wolfers decided to test the reaction to female economists in the US when they presented research. Women received 12 per cent more questions than men, which were more likely to be disruptive, patronising or hostile.[31] The research did trigger some action, with conference organisers banning interruptions for a speaker's first few minutes at the podium.

Along with a credibility deficit, women also encounter a credibility discount when they give evidence or make claims. It operates across society, with women's testimony about domestic violence and workplace harassment (more on this in Chapter 3) treated less favourably in courtrooms. The credibility discount operates at every step of the legal process. Or to put it another way, a woman's word is not taken as seriously as a man's.

When it comes to leadership, women not only have to work harder to prove themselves, but there's strong evidence to suggest they are more likely to get the top job during tough times. The work of Professor Michelle Ryan (mentioned in Chapter 1) on the famous 'glass cliff' research (with colleague Alex Haslam) describes a phenomena where women and people from other out-of-power groups have been disproportionately appointed to leadership roles at times of upheaval – and have therefore been more likely to fail.

I remember when I first read this study in 2008 with a growing sense of recognition. I'd seen a number of women appointed to tough jobs and then get criticised for not performing well, with their gender painted as the main culprit. The trend seems to be underpinned by women being seen as better at bringing the team together and tidying up the mess (sounds remarkably like parenting skills). In most of these cases, their tenure was followed by the appointment of what was seen as a 'steady pair' of hands – male hands. Glass cliff examples are rife in political leadership including the appointment of Julia Gillard after the deposing of Kevin Rudd, and former UK prime minister Theresa May.

It's not hard to find examples of a poisoned chalice when women step into leadership. While writing this book, a new CEO took the helm of Australia's iconic airline, Qantas. Former CEO Alan Joyce was replaced by Vanessa Hudson, the CFO and a 28-year veteran of the company. Media commentary about the change had a distinct whiff of glass cliff to it. The job for Hudson, many said, was mending the airline, restoring trust and fixing its poor customer relations. While her experience in keeping the company afloat during the pandemic was acknowledged, some questioned whether she had relied on Joyce to navigate the tough times. Perhaps this tone would have emerged in coverage about a male successor, perhaps not. It was also reported that Hudson's base pay would be $1.6 million compared to the $2 million base that Joyce started on 15 years before. Sometimes the numbers say it all.

The glass cliff can be a danger in any sector, even where women dominate as employees. Retailers in the US have been more likely to appoint men as CEOs with the number of women to take the corner office in 2023 dropping to five out of 47 CEOs, according to consumer expert Pamela Danziger and analysis by Korn Ferry. Twelve women leaving these jobs were replaced by men, and women CEOs had much shorter tenure in the role than men.[32] A study of the turnover and gender phenomena across a range of sectors, 'You're fired! Gender disparities in CEO dismissal,' from researchers at the University of Alabama's Culver College of Business, found that women have a 45 per cent greater likelihood of being fired than men, regardless of the firms' overall performance.

While the glass cliff is sadly still a trap for women, its

focus shouldn't only be on how it has an impact on them or the extra burdens they face, as Michelle Ryan has pointed out. A review of the glass cliff with her colleagues suggests that cushy leadership positions given disproportionately to men – a 'glass cushion' – could be part of the problem.[33] 'Focusing on women's disadvantage may also lead us to ignore men's privilege and advantage', she explained, and telling women to mimic men was not the solution. While it's no panacea, turning attention from women leaders' perceived failures to the problems with stereotypical male behaviour is definitely gathering pace.

The tolerance toll

Poor behaviour at the top is coming in for some extra scrutiny these days, with CEOs and politicians much less likely to get away with bullying behind the scenes. Changes in expectations combined with greater transparency through social media, and pressure from investors for better governance and gender outcomes, has made it much harder to get away with bad form at the top.

I've often reported on these cases and, in the past, noted the tolerance granted to men with high levels of chutzpah and 'big personalities' but questionable track records or behaviour. The 2022 sacking of James Hardie CEO Jack Truong for poor behaviour (which he denied) 'triggered a $1 billion fall in the company's market value' and followed 'the departure of CEOs from ASX-listed groups Oil Search, Cleanaway and Polynovo after concerns were raised internally about their management style', noted journalist Patrick Hatch.[34]

David Jones CEO Mark McGuiness was another example: a favourite in the business world, despite alleged problems with his behaviour to women, he eventually left his job in 2010 after saying he'd behaved in a manner unbecoming of a CEO. He got another CEO job a few months later. The same largesse is rarely granted to women who blot their copybook.

As I've noted, credibility and gravitas are still much more readily assumed for men (though not so much for non-white men). Obviously, tallness and a deep voice help, too. Men with privileged backgrounds, even with mediocre skills and experience, can more easily ascend hierarchies because they look and sound the part. I recall speaking at a corporate diversity event about the famous Malcolm Gladwell 'tall man' research, which found one-third of US CEOs were over 6 feet 2 inches tall, but only about 3 per cent of the male US population was that height. I glanced at the front row of the audience to find the very tall CEO of the company staring at me. I quickly moved on.

The assumption that men are more likely to know what they are talking about even extends to the topic of women's experience in the workplace. Former Australian prime minister Scott Morrison famously faced an interview in 2020 during yet another crisis over the treatment of women in parliament, with social services minister Anne Ruston at his side. When Ruston was asked what it was like for a woman in parliament, she barely got a sentence out before Morrison interrupted her. This truly epic manterruption made headlines around the country.

Women setting the course

At the heart of many of these prejudices and double standards faced by women is the tenacious idea that they are hardwired for caring not authority – that they don't fit into formal power structures, whether they are parents or not. Luckily, women are increasingly ignoring this well-worn story and changing the ground rules. It is usually when more women are at the decision-making table that bias in workplace rules and practices are addressed, and policies to blend caring and paid work are developed. For example, it was women leaders from academia, business, unions, community groups and government who were instrumental in efforts to finally legislate PPL.

Thanks to having these leaders, the focus is beginning to turn to the critical importance of putting those caregiving skills and the immense economic value of carers on the national agenda. I interviewed former director and business executive Sam Mostyn in late 2023, several months before she was appointed as Australia's Governor-General. I asked her about the speech she made on the key role of the care economy to the National Press Club in 2021. It laid out a clear case for disrupting the traditional economic story that ignores the impact of valuing essential care work – paid and unpaid. A couple of years after that agenda-setting speech, she explained to me that getting the policy settings to move fast enough and creating a big enough incentive for men to be carers, and active parents, is a priority. And that's where we'll see a change in who takes on care and responsibility, and pays the economic price for it, she told me.

But that's a long set of things that have to happen in the early education space, and with proper paid parental leave with super, and increasing parental leave to replacement wages, not just the minimum wage. We know that once you do and once men start taking caring roles too, it helps.

There's much more to be done in disrupting rigid ideas about caring, parental leave and flexibility, but it doesn't have to take a century, as is sometimes predicted. The pandemic showed us that the way we work can pivot fast. It's encouraging to note that while WFH remains under negotiation for many, there's a broader discussion unfolding about working hours, and a focus internationally on the benefits of a four-day work week, which some organisations such as KPMG are trialling. The ANU research on the glass-hours ceiling I mentioned also concluded that adjusting expectations of average work hours in countries like Finland has seen less of a gap between the weekly hours worked (40 for men and 38 for women) and better results than Australia on a range of gender-equality outcomes.

I've watched with some optimism as the new era triggered by PPL means more women access paid parenting leave and keep paid jobs. Now this template for change must go further. Gender bias continues to hamper women, but after examining the latest evidence, it's obvious it remains a major stumbling block for leadership before, after and even without child-bearing. It reinforces men as the natural bosses – the taller the better. Changing these beliefs need more than recognition, however. It's about overcoming two related stumbling blocks examined in the next chapters: the resistance and backlash that no one wants to talk about; and the way a heroic masculine leader is still often held up as the gold standard of leadership in media, case studies and management teaching.

Chapter 3

Tackling the elephant in the room: Backlash

The image of the Royal Spanish Football Federation president Luis Ribiales clasping the face of footballer Jenni Hermoso to kiss her after the final of the 2023 Women's World Cup (WWC) is unlikely to fade from memory quickly. Rubiales said the kiss was consensual, although Hermoso disagreed – which makes for an odd version of consensus. Hermoso was soon branded by a vocal cohort as a troublemaker who misinterpreted an innocent gesture, although many in Spain and around the world were appalled. Despite the attention paid to Kissgate (as it was soon dubbed), Ribiales initially refused to resign and blamed 'false feminism' and a witch hunt for the uproar. He eventually announced his resignation after a discussion with his daughters.

The incident was a jarring end to a myth-busting tournament featuring Australia's pin-up team, the Matildas. Years of scepticism were overturned by this display of power, skill, popularity and commercial clout. While men and women were enthusiastic fans of the WWC, the sheer success of the display must have rattled the cage of some of the men still firmly in charge of the game. Former Matilda and FIFA committee member Moya Dodd told the 2023 Women in Media conference that the tournament revealed two profound forces: the technical skill of the players and the misogyny of the governing ranks of the game.

It was a reminder that backlash to women's progress has some hallmarks: minimising, scoffing, blaming women and out of control 'woke' agendas. For all the talk of equity and opportunity, there's often a fierce response when women challenge powerful men. These ugly reactions are often explained away as aberrations, and the work of a bad apple, which makes defining and addressing backlash all the harder. But it's an essential step for accelerating women into leadership.

Yet those public reactions are probably the tip of the iceberg. Analysing the recent data about men's attitudes to gender equity reveals part of the story on why backlash has continued or even escalated, particularly in younger age groups. I also had a series of conversations with men – academics, experts and business leaders – about what back-lash looks like, why it happens, and how to address the problem.

Backlash and passive resistance to steps supporting women tends to come from a cohort of men with traditional attitudes about who does the work and care, and whose identity is framed by stereotypical masculine norms. This is a group that can be in denial about denial: they struggle to see their advantage as anything but natural and earned. As the sayings go, privilege is invisible to those who have it, and when you're accustomed to privilege, equality feels like oppression.

Blockers, resistors, minimisers, and denialists about sex-ism exist in many workplaces, and are insidiously effective in sowing seeds of doubt, defending inertia and derailing women's access to authority. I've lost count of how many times I've been told you have to be a woman to get on a board these days. When a recently retired male lawyer firmly explained this to me at a drinks event, the businessman standing next to him nodded in furious agreement: this was not only self-evident but horribly unfair, they believed. When I asked where they got their evidence from, and mentioned the still very low number of women on boards, they looked confused. Their perception was wildly exaggerated. Turns out the retiree has been unsuccessfully looking for a directorship, and decided the problem can't be him, so it must be less talented women to blame.

These beliefs about women 'getting away with it' are hard to measure and easy to deny. But anecdotal feedback from specialists suggests it remains common at even the most powerful echelons. There's still lots of belief that if it's good for women, it's bad for men, director and former Mirvac CEO Susan Lloyd-Hurwitz told me. She thinks that's an entirely false supposition, and women's partici-pation in the workforce is the single biggest lever we have to generate wealth and GDP in this country, which is good for everybody.

But I think [this win/lose belief] is still very much perceived as well. You've got an advantage because you're a woman. That's why you're on these boards. I had somebody say to me, 'Oh you're on the Rio Tinto board, it was because they were looking for women', which is an incredibly insulting thing.

Eye-wateringly sexist comments to one of Australia's most experienced executives are just part of the backlash story. While it's always been around, there's been an increase in particular forms of male resistance to women's truth telling, according to Professor Michael Flood from Queensland University of Technology, whose research focus is on gender, sexuality and interpersonal violence. This manifests in how women are depicted as lying or false accusers, he explained to me, with the 2023 National Community Attitudes Survey finding significantly more respondents believing women make false accusations. This may well be a reaction to women increasingly speaking out about sexual harassment, and the #MeToo movement, but other factors are at play.

> I do wonder whether it's been fuelled by particular online communities, anti-feminist or misogynist online communities, where the notion of women as false accusers is an article of faith? And I think those groups and networks are having some broader impacts on community receptiveness to that idea. So part of it is a really ancient story about women as liars and part of it, it's new and it's been quite actively disseminated particularly online.

This definitely includes younger men, too. As Flood pointed out, research shows men in their late 20s and 30s are much more willing to deny gender inequality and to adopt a series of sexist claims than men in their 40s and 50s.[1] In fact, global research released in 2024 found that women in their 20s were becoming more progressive and men less so in many countries around the world, with Australia reflecting this trend.[2] Flood told me there's a cohort of men now entering or in their first decade or so in workplaces, whose attitudes are significantly less progressive than those of older cohorts. Influencers like Andrew Tate and others were popular among young men, because they preach personal growth, and ways to make money, get fit and attract women, he said. But alongside sometimes problematic messages of self-improvement and personal growth, they also preach a toxic or really sexist mindset about women, and about feminism.

Meanwhile, several studies show a much larger group of men than women are sceptics about the existence of gender bias and believe there's been too much attention paid to it. In the world of paid work, one of the main reasons there's a default to over-optimism (see Chapter 1) and inertia has been because of these beliefs. Action to address sexism can run into high levels of resistance and even anger. But pretending backlash doesn't exist is making things worse. It lets alarmist rumours flourish about jobs, pay rises and promotions going to women without 'merit', or the folly of 'wasting' money on gender programs and addressing the pay gap.

Aggrieved resistance and cries of 'It's not fair' aren't confined to the workplace, but infiltrate relationships and families, too. I've heard time and again from women whose husbands, brothers and sons get angry and defensive about the push for gender equity, and complain they will miss out on promotions from this unwelcome competition. Although it's less common, sometimes women agree with these reservations. This isn't surprising given the messaging women receive most of their lives about men being expected and entitled to be the main breadwinners. When women defend sexism, and resort to victim blaming, it's sometimes the result of 'internalised misogyny' from absorbing the narrative about traditional gender stereotypes, particularly about who should be the boss.

But more often I've heard stories of the shock when a woman finds her male partner or relative isn't exactly on board with gender equity. A young women approached me after I spoke at a women's leadership conference for a local government group. That morning as she was leaving home, her boyfriend had asked what she was doing during the day. When she told him about the event, he aggressively responded that attending a women's event 'wasn't fair'. What about conferences for men? he asked her. She was unimpressed, which probably didn't bode well for their relationship. Of course, she was actually spending the day hearing how to navigate these kinds of attitudes and barriers to get her job done. Meanwhile, he would no doubt be unlikely to have his views challenged, (except by her, of course) but quite possibly reinforced by his peers.

The majority of Australians (90 per cent) actually believe gender equity is important.[3] But the reality is that drilling down into men's attitudes reveals progress has stalled. A surprisingly large cohort are ambivalent at best and some believe they are being discriminated against. It seems Australian men's attitudes to gender equity are more traditional than many other comparable economies, and closer to those in Malaysia, China and Poland according to research released in 2022.[4] The data found that in Australia, 30 per cent of men agreed that gender inequality didn't really exist, which put the country at seventh out of 30 nations; and 32 per cent of men agreed that men have lost out in terms of economic or political power or socially because of feminism.

Half of people worldwide still believe men make better political leaders than women, and more than 40 per cent believe men make better business executives than women according to the UN's 2023 Gender Social Norms Index (GSNI) report.[5] A staggering 25 per cent of people worldwide believe it is justified for a man to beat his wife. The trend isn't uplifting: there's been no improvement in biases against women in a decade, with almost 9 out of 10 men and women worldwide still holding such biases today.

In workplaces, the resistance and disbelief about gender inequity is reflected in the gap between men's and women's perception of the topic, even when there is clear evidence of bias. A survey released in 2021 found men and women in finance and insurance jobs had vastly different opinions on the transparency and equity in their workplaces, according to the Financial Services Institute of Australia.[6] The findings showed even fewer women believed their organisation was committed in practice to the advancement of women into senior roles than the previous survey in 2018.

As I wrote at the time, it was not so much a gap in views as a chasm – particularly when it came to the gender pay gap.[7] A staggering 77 per cent of the men responding to the study were neutral, agreed or strongly agreed that the pay gap was grossly exaggerated, despite the sector having one of the widest gender pay gaps in Australia at the time: around 27.5 per cent. Only 40 per cent of women felt the same way. Nearly three times more men (58 per cent) agree their employer is transparent about remuneration, compared to 18 per cent of women. Such a difference could be a case of wilful blindness or just plain ignorance, but the fact so many men remain unconvinced these problems exist at all despite years of data gathering is pretty disturbing. And these are people who make a living crunching numbers.

There's a related issue – and resistance to change – revealed by data collected by Workplace Gender Equality Agency (WGEA) on gender pay gap audits. While 54 per cent of reporting organisations say they have done an audit, just 40 per cent of that group have taken action to address the findings. When I interviewed WGEA director Mary Wooldridge she said the main reason for the failure to act was also revealing.

Three-quarters say the reason they haven't taken any action is there's no unexplained or unjustifiable gaps. So it's that sense of, 'Well, it just confirmed everything I know. I'm in, let's say, the construction sector and you know, we have a lot of men and they've been around for a long time, and therefore, I don't do anything about it, because that's exactly what I expected to see'. And that's the nature of the structure of the industry.

So, the overwhelming response is that is why they don't do it, they have ticked the box. And, there's no easy fix. And I think there's probably a combination of not wanting to and not feeling able to lead or be part of the structural changes that need to happen to fundamentally change the nature of what you would always expect. So the stereotypes are reinforced, the numbers tell them that. That's exactly what they expected: it's just the way it is.

A few months after I spoke to Mary Wooldridge, WGEA published the gender pay gap details for more than 5000 individual organisations for the first time. The headline-grabbing revelations showed 62 per cent of employers had a gap over 5 per cent in favour of men.[8] This included significant gaps among household names: Qantas, BHP, Commonwealth Bank, and even women's sports clothing company Lorna Jane. Of course, most of these organisations already knew what their pay gap was because they have been collecting the data for years. But sunlight is said to be the best disinfectant, and seeing those percentages across the media sparked a welcome acknowledgement to do better from some employers.

But others relied on excuses or blamed women for 'choosing' to do the caring or failing to ask for a raise. Some organisations stated the obvious, by pointing out that the gap arose because there were more men in senior jobs who take home the big pay packets – which is indeed the key reason for the gap and where change is needed. In fact, looking at the data, it was clear this is not only a gender pay gap but a gender power gap.

The aim of this public airing is to focus the minds of employers on doing more than box ticking, and start addressing the causes of the gap. In the UK, where a similar regime came into effect in 2017, the gender pay gap hasn't disappeared, but more employers have taken steps to address it. But the initial Australian reaction also included some commentary, particularly on social media, denying the gap really exists or that women face disadvantage. This scepticism will no doubt continue despite the evidence.

Denial of the gender pay gap is actually closely linked to

another stark difference between men and women, revealed by FINSIA. It found that men were also much less likely to know how few women were in management or on boards of their organisations (another example of over-optimism). Men in the sector were more likely to believe there was a 50/50 split of gender in most parts of their organisations, when the actual figure in management and senior jobs is more like 30 per cent (and just 10 per cent of CEOs are women).[9]

It's important to tackle this piece of fiction because if there were just as many women as men executives and they were paid appropriately, there wouldn't be a gender pay gap (which is usually calculated as the difference in weekly average full-time earnings between men and women). It's also really a gender leadership gap, says University of South Australia's Professor Carol Kulik. The pay gap reflects the large number of women clustered in low-paid and low-skilled jobs in many organisations and sectors. But calls to make this dynamic clearer are possibly not helping because of a tendency to defend the status quo and resist the idea that sexism is to blame, she told me.

> I think we no longer have community support for reducing gender bias. One of my current interests is specifically around gender pay gaps. And I sometimes hear, 'if people understood the gender pay gap, they would be outraged'. I actually think it's the opposite. I think the more people understand the gender pay gap, the less outraged they become. Because it's not about like-for-like jobs, it's about occupational segregation. It's about career gaps due to child rearing.

And this is where the community says, 'Oh, so it's all a woman's choice'. That's a really big factor: we don't have community support. We don't have community outrage. We don't have moral indignation to fuel the movement.

If you believe women are just predisposed to work in lower paid and lower skilled jobs, and you fear losing out from more competition, then you're much more likely to deny or resist steps to tackle sexism. That's risky, Kulik says. Organisations that have gender pay gaps within their executive team fail to leverage gender diversity, with negative consequences for financial performance. The bottom-line impact shows that resistance to acknowledging and addressing the gender pay gap isn't just causing problems for women; it's a problem for their employers. The research gives organisations a very practical reason to take pay gaps – and resistance to them – seriously.

Underestimating the gender pay gap is also fed by the belief that the workplace operates fairly and everyone gets ahead on 'merit'. Women with merit, the thinking goes, will be automatically recognised in exactly the same way as men are. We've done nowhere near enough to break down the notion that until now we've had a level playing field, Flood noted. And the notion that women are now unfairly getting ahead is perhaps particularly on the radar for some men, who struggle to accept the idea that their achievement in workplaces hasn't actually all been the result of superior skills. No wonder steps to address bias and discrimination for this group can feel an awful lot like unfairness.

In fact, the failure to deliver better gender outcomes actually suggests there's been too little, not too much, action. A lack of progress then leaves managers feeling unmotivated, as a 2023 global study by staffing firm Kelly found. DEI (diversity, equity and inclusion) initiatives by corporations have plateaued and may be dropping off – a sign of DEI fatigue.

> Nearly half of executives (45%) recognise that their DEI strategy does not adequately support under-represented groups. Shockingly, fewer than one in five (14%) executives say their organisation has a clear route for reporting discrimination at work. Employees are divided, with 46% of talent saying that leaders in their organisation model inclusive behaviours at all times, while the other half (49%) believe their employer does not support DEI enough.[10]

In the US, backlash has been blamed for reversing a trend that saw appointments of DEI managers at a range of organisations during the pandemic and after the Black Lives Matter movement. Large corporations such as Disney have cut the role, with some observers saying more cuts are to come because 'leaders don't view these roles, and indeed diversity, as imperative to business success'.[11]

Some of this trend may also be due to the US Supreme Court overturning of race-conscious admissions programs in higher education. This means that colleges and institutions are no longer able to take race into account when deciding which qualified candidates will be admitted. Even though the Supreme Court ruling was for higher education, it has started to have an impact across US businesses, which might be more inclined to review diversity programs and targets.

This backtracking on programs and lack of serious DEI commitment seems, at best, premature. When it comes to addressing gender inequity there's often been a tendency for less rigour, a preoccupation with the latest trend, and lack of accountability or goals. Backlash and scepticism thrive when there's a reliance on superficial remedies that don't deliver. Unconscious bias is certainly a well-documented phenomenon, but putting employees through a short session on it usually doesn't fix the problem. It turns out many people who attend these forums have their biases confirmed because they feel there's nothing they can do about them.

Box ticking and DEI lip service from leaders are effective roadblocks to addressing backlash. I interviewed an experienced Australian DEI manager (who prefers to remain anonymous) and was told that trying to get action by senior leadership required 'diversity by stealth'. The longer this specialist worked in the area, and had detailed conversations with CEOs, the more it became apparent that the boss mostly wanted to outsource any action so they didn't have to do anything themselves. Senior leaders have little reason to change the status quo, and fear backlash from peers. But an effective DEI manager is doing much more than running the occasional women's development training course, the specialist said.

> We're coming in there to deconstruct the way that
> you think about leadership so that women who were
> working hard and are amazing can become leaders

within that system. That is absolutely not what (CEOs) were signing up for. So you spend most of your time as DEI practitioner doing harm reduction and harm minimisation. You're not going to go to the people who run the system and tell them what they need is to change the system that benefits them ... there's absolutely zero chance of that happening.

This failure of leaders to prioritise DEI and prevent backlash is supported by research from the Australian Human Resources Institute.[12] The vast majority (84 per cent) of HR professionals say that DEI is critical to the future success of their organisation. However, only half (50 per cent) of HR professionals say that their leaders see it as a priority for their organisation, while a similar proportion (49 per cent) also say that their organisation is not placing enough focus on DEI.

I've done many interviews with CEOs about this topic and while they talked up their credentials, most didn't want to upset the apple cart for fear of backlash. But it's often easy for men to deny they are part of the problem, says Matthew Byrne, an Australian Graduate School of Management Program Director, adjunct faculty and former executive. He's been running the General Manager five-day leadership program for AGSM for the last seven years and it's given him some insights into how gender dynamics play out, particularly among groups of men at a mid-career stage.

He tells every group that it's time for men to start changing and liberating themselves. Most participants are either stunned or irritated by this suggestion. But moving men from traditional stereotypes to a new model is a valid topic and has to at least have the potential to tackle rather than ignite backlash, he explains.

> My whole purpose is to create a psychologically safe space to have the conversation about white male entitlement. That's how all my programs have always finished, and giving the space for the men to have a reflective conversation about it and to listen to women to talk about their truths. And to understand that those truths are still very different. And that is a surprise and shock to most participants, and men in particular.

> When I'm talking about that with men, they [say] they want women to succeed but not at their own expense. And I am saying, 'How do you define at your expense? If you want to be the next CEO and a woman gets there in front of you, is that because she is a woman, and she's been a diversity pick so it is easy to dismiss her as no good and she has no idea what she's doing?' That's 1990s thinking.

This concern about women getting ahead unfairly often stems from the idea that any steps supporting women will inevitably penalise men, as director Susan Lloyd-Hurwtiz has pointed out. There's not really much evidence supporting this zero-sum equation, but that hasn't stopped it circulating.

It was spelled out by former Australian prime minister Scott Morrison at an International Women's Day event some years ago when he said it was important women didn't get ahead 'at the expense of others'. It's an understatement to observe it didn't quite strike the right note. But it accurately reflects the attitudes of a significant group. US data from the Pew Research Center 'shows that around one in three American males believes that the gains women have made towards society becoming more gender-equal have come at the expense of men'.[13]

That said, there is some truth to part of this rationale. After all, if you have been part of a system where your gender, class and race gave you a distinct advantage, then you might be shocked to find that's less often the case. But at least acknowledging this reality, putting it in context (most men are still unlikely to lose their job because there are more women in the workplace), and dealing with those who are aggrieved by the changes in social and workplace norms would be a wise first step, as some CEOs explain a little later.

Specialist DEI adviser Roman Ružbacký firmly believes senior men need to step up to tackle backlash. After spending decades advising organisations about how to make gender equity progress, he explained to me that many men at the top have a combination of low consciousness; low competency; intentionality to keep the status quo; lack of action; no lived experience; a failure to acknowledge intersectionality; and applaud mediocre tokenism. Many aren't really engaging, educating themselves or getting the expertise that is needed. Their power is still blinding them to what marginalised employees are facing.

> It seems that we are always placing the onus on
> marginalised individuals to continually raise concerns
> in organisations or speak about their lived experience

of inequity at forums, when many men in power don't have the same pressure.

Many of the gender equity action plans I have written over the years contain anywhere from 20 to even 70 actions, spanning three to four years. This can be overwhelming for any leader of an organisation or DEI executive champion, as they feel the expectation to complete an additional 50 tasks on top of their already busy schedule. I have designed these action plans as a guide that helps them to do their work better and contemplate gender equity and inclusion principles in everything they do. Many of the actions in plans are also connected and real skill is required to practise gender equity work intuitively.

This would be easier if diversity wasn't often viewed as a bolt on to HR practices or something that's 'nice to have' but not essential. It helps to make it clear that sexism isn't only about extreme forms of harassment. Everyday sexism falls into two broad categories: hostile sexism that justifies men's power and traditional gender roles through negative characterisation of women; and benevolent sexism that appears kinder, and uses paternalism and gentler justifications of power, according to Michael Flood.[14] This manifests in the denial of continued discrimination against women, negative reactions to complaints about inequality, and resistance to efforts addressing sexism.

Denial of gender bias is a particular problem in some surprising sectors – I've mentioned how it plays out in the start-up space, and in science and medicine as the examples about vets and doctors in Chapter 1 show. Cancer researcher UNSW Professor Caroline Ford says gender bias is a fraught area for highly intelligent scientists who pride themselves on sticking to the facts. When you try to talk to them about bias or inequity, they take umbrage because they are so horrified to think that they could be doing something perceived as wrong or dumb. Tackling the problem is about showing that science is biased because it's done by scientists – who are people, she adds. They bring their own biases and culture to that job, and they are being asked to recognise those and that there are flaws in the system.

I asked a couple of men in CEO roles about handling backlash as they introduced a range of practices to boost women's participation in the workplace. CEO of construction company Multiplex, John Flecker, told me most steps to introduce flexibility or get more women onto decision-making boards (see the case study on the Australian Constructors Association Board in Chapter 6) don't usually run into resistance. But the area where he finds backlash emerges is the perception that women will get promoted over men without similar experience.

The only area I ever get pushback is the old 'Well, it's all good. But if Candidate A is a male who is more capable than Candidate B, then I don't really like the idea of candidate B being leapfrogged over candidate A because she's female'. And that leads into a whole other debate about 'Well, how do we change if we don't change?' But that gets harder. And I don't think that people are saying that out of not wanting females to succeed, or for us to improve gender diversity. But we sort of have this equity struggle. And that's where you're getting into the more granular areas.

Similarly, in 2018 Scott Wyatt, CEO of Viva Energy and a member of the Champions of Change Coalition (a group of around 250 CEOs committed to gender equity and increasing the number of women in leadership), began to look at ways to attract women into the male-dominated fuel refinery and delivery business. There was reluctance from some quarters. When we really got serious about this, he recalled, it was quite difficult conversations at the senior levels around it because no one felt comfortable with targets. There was the normal stuff about getting the best people for the job, and needing to tread softly at first, but then he made some determined changes in a range of these areas (outlined in Chapter 6). Then people do see the real benefits of that change, because it's hard not to, he told me. 'You go to the refinery now and you walk around, it's visibly different. And there's lots of other things we've done around culture there as well. But the elements of diversity, and gender diversity particularly, has been a big part of changing the culture.'

That change can also come from everyday interventions. Gavin Fox-Smith, CEO of healthcare company Omnigon and also a Champions of Change Coalition member, told me about how the norms around treatment of women can start with ignoring incidents or behaviour when I interviewed him for a story on addressing sexism and sexual harassment.[15] Years ago, he recalled, there was an introductory forum at a company he'd just joined, and coffees were ordered and left outside the boardroom.

Who gets up to get the coffees? The woman in the room. A director and owner of the company and one of the most senior people. Not one man moved, and I got the coffees and walked back in and stopped the meeting and said, 'One of the things I'm going to do is, I don't expect women to get the coffee in the boardroom', and you should have seen how uncomfortable some of these men got. And to me, that small example meant I was able to talk about gender equality by doing it in a real live session – they got it immediately … all of us as leaders need to say we are comfortable to do that.

The failure to act is not due to a lack of levers or programs, he said. The tools are all there, and in the majority of well-run companies, there were sexual harassment policies and reporting mechanisms. But many leaders still don't get the impact of these behaviours and their responsibility to address them.

Backlash may not completely disappear if the boss is prioritising diversity, but it can dissipate. It's also easier for men to step up as allies and actually join networks and conversations about diversity instead of letting it continue to be seen as women's business. Just about every event I speak at or attend on this topic has an overwhelmingly female audience. Gender, it appears, isn't something a lot of men think they have. Leaving the entire diversity debate on women's shoulders is clearly not going to shift the power structure or help address backlash.

'Women in senior roles are twice as likely as men at their level to take time doing DEI work outside their formal responsibilities, and women at all levels are taking most of the actions of allyship', according to coach and Forbes contributor Sheila Goldgrab.[16] Men who want to shift the dial should also be giving women fair credit for their work and contribution (instead of mansplaining to them, as I've noted):

> Encouraging allies to elevate the accomplishments of women by bringing them out of obscurity and making them visible to the right people when their co-worker is not there is an act of male allyship. So is stepping forward to call out those who over-emphasize their role and eclipse the contributions of others. Giving credit is a vital part of the competencies required for good teamwork, collaboration, and developing and attracting top talent. It's good leadership.[17]

It can be much easier to claim you are an ally than actually do something about it, with research showing that men think they are supporting women colleagues but often do it quietly or out of sight.[18] But when men support and highlight the accomplishments of women instead of questioning them, they can have enormous impact.

It's also helpful if men back women supporting women. I've researched the widespread phenomenon of networks that women build (*Women Kind* with Kirstin Ferguson[19]). It's a trend at odds with the enduring Queen Bee clichés and cultural 'mean girl' tropes suggesting women are particularly prone to stab each other in the back. From mothers' groups to book clubs and industry groups, women join and obviously find support from these forums. But they often run into ridicule or worse for sticking up for each other in the workplace and can be accused of 'playing the gender card'. When men take the initiative and vouch for women, instead of belittling or making fun of their efforts, they might cop some ribbing, but there's also a chance it reflects well on them. And men often support or vouch for each other without a qualm – and to great effect.

Sometimes men in particular have a light-bulb moment when there's time spent making the case for change and allaying fears about gender equity. A program on male allyship called Step Up, developed by the Coles Group in conjunction with consultancy People Measures, was really well received by the male participants, former deputy chair of gender equity group The 100% Project, and Coles senior finance manager, Laura Innes told me.

The facilitator, Frances Feenstra, gave me an example of one man who said, 'Well, I don't see the lack of gender equity really kind of applies to me, I've done everything that I can'. And by the end of it, he said: 'Oh, wow, I can see how I maybe could have been contributing to this and it makes me want to think about that and do something differently'. So I think in the past, we've all been so focused on fixing the woman. Now it's 'how do we change a system designed by men and run by men?' How can we get more men involved and to play more of an active role in diversity and inclusion? Because we've got to - it's got to change for all genders and I think that's one of the things quite relevant for people in power: what does that mean for them? If we are getting more

women in those senior positions, does that mean
there's less opportunities for those young men?

Flushing out the unspoken elements of resistance and
educating men on gender data has the potential to make
them active allies – and that makes a very big difference
to outcomes, according to research in the public sector by
Carol Kulik and colleagues. They examined the effect of
targets and whether more women appointed at the top leads
to a 'trickle down' effect (more on this in Chapter 6) of
better outcomes for women throughout the ranks. Turns out
that trickle down is contingent on a few factors. Sometimes
when targets are imposed the policies are not well supported
in practice, or deliberately blocked or resisted.[20]

In departments with a consistent trickle down, strong
visible support from the chief executive provided legitimacy
to implement interventions, even when there was resistance.
Where there was inconsistent trickle down, the chief
executive may have been supportive, but it was not explicit
and so blockers were able to disrupt champions' efforts.
Blockers operated throughout the public service, the study
found. If a department had gender champions, blockers
resisted their change efforts and reduced the champions'
impact by using both passive and active strategies.

The recent push for men to be active allies also helps
shift the focus off women taking steps to confront sexism.
That's crucial because women face daunting backlash for
speaking up, and the belief they are making up claims of
sexism. This was a regular refrain during the tenure of
former prime minister Julia Gillard, despite her stoic refusal
for nearly two years to formally address the appalling

sexism directed at her. She thought it would die away in due course, but it only gathered pace until she decided enough was enough. Her famous misogyny speech was greeted with relief and applause by many women around the world, but triggered immediate howls of outrage from some quarters and media commentators. Given the overt and toxic nature of what Gillard faced, the idea she was deflecting attention by making up excuses about bias were almost laughable.

I was astounded by how quickly the toxic sexist criticism and lack of respect for the prime minister was normalised. Colleagues of mine, experienced journalists who I had worked with for years, told me they felt some sympathy for Gillard initially, but then believed she brought the problem on herself. This reaction reminded me how slow, and often superficial, progress has been in tackling boss bias. By the time she delivered her speech, many women in Australia and internationally felt her anger was not so much an over-reaction as overdue.

Unfortunately, the suggestion that women exaggerate or make up stories about sexism do often hit the mark. Whistleblowers generally don't fare well for their efforts and can be earmarked as troublemakers or hounded from their jobs. Former AMP Capital director Julia Szlakowski, for example, spoke out about her experience at AMP, which eventually triggered an upheaval in the financial services company in 2017. The company promoted high-flyer Boe Pahari to run AMP Capital despite having penalised him $500000 following settlement of a sexual harassment complaint by Szlakowski. Fed up with platitudes about 'zero tolerance' for harassment, female AMP employees made their outrage clear. Pahari was demoted and eventually left the firm, with a severance said to be worth $50 million.

In a 2021 speech, Szlakowski outlined her experience since speaking out, and said companies that fail to properly handle complaints of sexual harassment let the harassed get punished all over again.

> Those of us who do decide to speak up almost never work in our chosen professions again … and I would be remiss not to mention that my experience would undoubtedly be exponentially worse if I still spoke with an accent, worked for minimum wage, lived in a non-democratic country, didn't have white skin, wasn't able-bodied, didn't possess a resilient mind or identified as anything other than heterosexual.[21]

Despite her testimony, the incident didn't result in widespread improvements in workplace behaviour or support for complainants. In fact, the AMP incident triggered backlash: in some business circles there was concern expressed that men would now be too nervous to have meetings alone with women. Former AMP director John Fraser told a podcast in 2020 that he took two middle-aged women with him to corporate social events to act as 'minders', although just who was needing protection is not clear.

No analysis of resistance in this arena can ignore that bastion of the patriarchy: the notorious network known as the boys' club. It's the brotherhood with no rules or formal membership criteria but enormous power and influence behind the scenes. It offers invaluable sponsorship, access and know-how to members – who are quick to close ranks when they are under threat. When it's called out for bolstering entitlement and sexism, it's often women who are told how to get around it or form their own version. That's not going to dismantle a system where power stays in the hands of an elite privileged group.

Groucho Marx famously quipped he wouldn't want to join a club that would have him as a member. There's certainly few powerful men advertising their connections to 'behind closed doors' bonding, so it is notoriously tricky to analyse. But some research does confirm that gender loyalty has a significant impact on who gets ahead, with men promoted more often by other men than by women. This 'male-to-male advantage' in promotions could account for 39 per cent of the gender gap in pay.[22]

In the Australian finance sector, embedded bias has played a role in forming and reinforcing men's networks, according to research by The 100% Project.[23] This could be due to the historically male workforce in the sector, which promotes affinity bias – the natural tendency to prefer, network and socialise with people who look like each other. This fosters the 'boys' club' culture and provides men with important career sponsorship while excluding women, causing them to miss out on important networking opportunities. Loyalty to the boys' club doesn't only operate at the top. Mateship is an iconic national value in Australia, with strong masculine connotations. While it has an important bonding role, mateship can be highly excluding if you don't happen to be part of the dominant cohort.

The cost of ignoring or failing to read the room on back-lash, the boys' club and everyday sexism isn't about hurt feelings or a victim mentality. It's a rapidly increasing reputational and bottom-line risk. Those incidents that might have raised not much more than an eyebrow in days gone by are regularly making headlines. An outright scandal erupted in NSW politics in 2022 when former MP John Barilaro was appointed to the lucrative New York trade commissioner role despite a recruitment process initially offering the job to a woman. A subsequent parliamentary inquiry found the process was flawed and 'had all the trademarks of a "job for the boys" position'. And media reports noted the 2023 birthday celebrations for Australian business figure Lindsay Fox, held at the National Gallery of Victoria, brought together 130 leaders to celebrate – almost all white men.

There's a wilful blindness in these cases to male responsibility for not just prevention but cure. Women are targeted with advice and defensive tactics, while men and particularly predatory behaviour seem to be left out of the equation. Luckily the occasional 'boys will be boys' defence is attracting plenty of pushback these days. The same goes for media reporting of violence against women with growing calls to stop portraying male perpetrators as 'good blokes' pushed to the edge.

While social norms are slowly shifting, action on backlash does require many more men to step out of their comfort zone and become allies, as both Ružbacký and Byrne point out. The men Byrne teaches are often very good at denying any collective responsibility for sexism or bias (which is where the #notallmen hashtag comes in). On the other hand, Australians are very good at taking collective responsibility for sporting success, such as winning an Olympic gold medal. When men say they are 'not like that' they are often absolving themselves from any role in recognising what their women peers confront. 'But men with goodwill and a real unease about gender inequity do want to find a way to speak up – and there's lots of us,' Byrne adds.

On the plus side, Michael Flood also notes that despite more younger men holding sexist attitudes, and using humour as an excuse for sexist cracks, they are unlikely to make overt remarks in many workplaces. There have been genuinely progressive shifts in workplace culture, and at least some sense of how sexual harassment or overtly sexist comments are inappropriate, he said.

When presenting to audiences on male advocacy and allyship, including at BHP and other corporates, Flood says it's also important to emphasise the positive: most men support the principle of gender equity, and they often over-estimate other men's tolerance for poor behaviour. It's about appealing to men as bystanders, and the need to speak up in the face of poor treatment of women, and inviting men to hold themselves to account as well.

For gender and leadership consultant and trans woman Sally Goldner, there's a couple of core prerequisites that she has seen make a big difference to becoming an effective ally.

Sometimes being an ally involves the humility to shut up and listen. And listening is often seen as a more 'feminine' quality. We're not taught how to listen. Sometimes when delivering training sessions, I'll talk about how many people in their first 18 years of life got any structured training in listening skills, and in a room of 20 I'll be lucky to get one. And, for women, they are – sadly of course – told they should just shut

up and do what they're told, and listen to the men.
And so coming back to allyship, it is that humility to
listen to someone else.

All these individual levers can counter backlash and resistance. But it's important to acknowledge more needs to be done to tackle institutionalised indifference and resistance to the evidence that shows the impact of better gender equity: the ubiquitous business case (see Chapter 1). In 2020 the Workplace Gender Equality Agency published a study showing a causal relationship between more women in senior ranks and bottom-line results.[24] It found that an increase in the share of female 'top-tier' managers by 10 percentage points or more led to a 6.6 per cent increase in the market value of Australian ASX-listed companies. It was the business case on steroids.

Instead of attracting headlines, the report was sidelined. Even allowing for the effect of COVID, the lack of reaction astounded Libby Lyons, director of WGEA at the time. It was the first time a longitudinal data set had found this causal link internationally, yet the response from media, organisations and industry bodies was pathetic and it just wasn't picked up, she told me. 'The whole reason we collect data is to get hard evidence about what works and what doesn't work, and it just fell on deaf ears.'

I hear this lip service, saying things like, 'We
need the data'. So we set up the agency, we get the
longitudinal data. We get the WGEA scorecard
every year. We see that progress is at a snail's pace.
We get the hard evidence of the fact that you put

more women in leadership, you get better business outcomes and yet this evidence is ignored. Every director and board in this country need to heed the hard evidence in this report and act, because if they do not, they are not upholding their ficuciary duties to their shareholders.

This silence in the face of strong evidence tells us a lot about the way denial, gender washing and scapegoating women still operates. I rarely hear demand for details of the business case at forums these days, despite or perhaps because of the compelling data. I'm a fan of data (obviously) but I've been getting increasingly fed up with being told women have to show they improve results so they can participate and progress in their own workplaces. There's no business case for the status quo, as I once heard a DEI expert dryly explain.

But that's not the only message from the WGEA report, which provides key information on how to boost more women in leadership. Ignoring world-leading research shows how much more effort is needed to effectively confront the uncomfortable reality that resistance and backlash obstruct action to address the barriers. As well as encouraging allies, getting men involved in initiatives and educating senior teams to take DEI policies seriously, there's a need to spell out the reputational and financial stakes when there's only lip service about women's progress and wilful blindness to the benefits. The risks of defending the status quo are already high – and only getting higher.

Chapter 4
Learning new leadership lessons

When Tesla's Elon Musk challenged Meta's Mark Zuckerberg to a cage fight in mid-2023, the ludicrous prospect attracted plenty of jibes – but didn't entirely jar. The idea started when the two traded barbs online and Musk challenged his competitor to an actual contest. The image of two powerful men clashing in hand-to-hand combat (with the Colosseum tipped as a potential venue) isn't too hard to conjure up. High-profile, authoritarian businessmen prone to hubris are far from rare – in fact, many still think that description is synonymous with leadership.

Look up 'leadership gurus' and Google helpfully sorts through millions of possible sources to show 24 profile pictures – all white and just one woman. Lists of top international management thinkers and profiles in leadership publications aren't exactly diverse either. You'll usually be hard put to find more than a handful of women (mostly white) prominently featured – if they are there at all. The top five leadership case studies used in many management courses and books often include Steve Jobs at Apple, and Musk at Tesla, and presumably as a warning, Elisabeth Holmes, the disgraced founder of Theranos. So much for gender equity measures going too far.

Of course, as this book makes clear, a lot of leaders are men. But there are outstanding women in leadership of all kinds, and many experts in academia, consulting and government. You really wouldn't know from a trawl through the annals, and that's a big problem. Women can only make meaningful progress into authority when there are new lessons and different role models that change the story about who has what it takes to be the boss.

As a veteran of leadership and management reporting, including more than a decade at *Boss* magazine (published by the Australian Financial Review), I've interviewed quite a few of the old-guard management and leadership stars. The roll call includes leadership academics and authors Tom Peters, John Kotter, Jim Collins, Michael Porter, business leaders Richard Branson and Jack Welch, and occasionally to my delight, some women: European Central Bank's Christine Lagarde and academic Rosabeth Moss Kanter.

With the exception of the latter, and occasionally Peters, their take on management and leadership has largely remained unruffled by the waves of women's rights activism and calls to address bias and discrimination. The same with some of the global business celebrities: it would be an exaggeration to say their interest in gender equity is lukewarm. It's almost as though women and serious leadership expertise are mutually exclusive. The heroic man has been the default leader for so long, anything else can still seem sacrilegious.

Sitting on a lofty pedestal, born not made, this masculine archetype underpins the courses, apps, workshops, skills frameworks and CEO profiles that are recycled to define the very principles of leadership and who is entitled to get to the top. Changing these parameters and removing the barriers to entry for women can't get far unless this biased and hugely influential framework is actively challenged and ultimately revamped.

I've seen the man-leader syndrome play out. Although *Boss* magazine, where I worked for many years, always featured female leaders and thinkers, the male quotient was much higher. When possible, the net was cast a little more widely, sometimes broadening the definition of leadership to include senior women who were not yet CEOs, or entrepreneurs. It brought a different group of leaders into contention instead of focusing on a small pool of executives and chairs of large organisations, which guaranteed few women or culturally diverse people would be featured.

All too often, the global leadership gurus we profiled were homogenous in appearance and thinking. I once interviewed one of these household name 'celebrity' business tycoons in a hotel lobby. During the entire exchange he avoided any eye contact with me while staring intently at any young women who happened to walk past, and flirting with a couple of his highly attractive employees. Much more problematic for me, however, were his interview responses which were, at best, predictable and uninspiring.

Interviewing the formidable Jack Welch was another memorable encounter. It's hard to exaggerate his guru status as CEO of GE at the time, with many in the business world keen to hear about, and emulate, his uncompromising formula for success. The interview was by phone before he was due to arrive in Australia for a speaking tour, with hordes queuing to hear about the approach that earned him the nickname Neutron Jack. At one stage this modus operandi included sacking the 'bottom' 10 per cent of GE employees annually. When I suggested that was not likely to work in an economy like Australia's, where getting enough staff is usually a challenge, the line suddenly went dead. It was 'my way or the highway' with Jack.

Welch is a good example of the Great Man syndrome, a term that was used by 19th-century philosopher Thomas Carlyle. Not all men were leaders but leaders were all men – and they were born that way, according to Carlyle. Australian director and author Kirstin Ferguson, one of the few women to write a popular leadership book, says the term 'leader' has been associated with men for centuries.[1] 'Most of us learn about leaders at school or university, and they were titans of industry, kings or explorers or generals on the battlefield,' she pointed out. This means that leadership theorists have mostly homed in on ways to emulate the qualities of this cohort. This was reflected in the early MBA programs, and how we thought about the components of leadership: a focus on strategy, business excellence and technical expertise.

There have been more efforts to showcase diverse leadership in the media, and as leadership gurus, in recent times. However, the gender problem remains endemic. There's still a default in management literature and leadership courses to male norms and role models, which then reinforce these traditional qualities. As the slow realisation of this in-built bias and reinforcement from moribund leadership lessons emerges, 'the template laid down by and for very different people and conditions more than half a century ago has started to chafe', writes journalist Simon Calkin. It's companies and their leadership that need to adapt to women and not the other way around, he writes.[2]

'The current position isn't desirable, and probably not

sustainable either', Harvard Business School (HBS) professor Amy Edmondson, specialist in teams and organisational learning, told Calkin. 'I don't think men have a monopoly on obsolete management mindsets, but they probably tend to hold them more often, and by that, I mean the core idea that fear and command and control is the way you get things done.' In fact these old norms, which value force over collaboration and innovation, come at a cost and have probably allowed far too many mediocre men into leadership.

Business schools' curricula can reinforce male leadership styles with the occasional bolted-on women's leadership module. There's a tendency to promote the virtues of so-called soft skills in theory, but fewer examples of it in practice or in case studies. Those business and political heroes who are most often lauded are rarely collegiate types. Meanwhile the lucrative coaching and leadership training sector (with some exceptions) tends to fit in with the cultural norms equating masculinity with leadership. This is actually reinforced in the reams of advice particularly targeting women (see Chapter 5) about how to make it into leadership. It tends to promote imitating a male version of confidence, or reinforces a stoic and uncomplaining style that fits in, but does not disrupt power dynamics.

These biases also influence the kinds of practical tools and training used in organisations, and the diversity research and advice from high-profile consultancies such as McKinsey and Boston Consulting Group. I've spoken to several CEOs who have conceded privately that consulting advice on improving gender equity has lots of data but often recycles a series of approaches. One former CEO told me he was looking for practical guidance on diversity measures during his tenure and read a lot of the strategic consulting firms' reports about diversity. He found there were a couple of things that struck him: 'One is, if you go back far enough reading McKinsey and Bain and BCG, you'll find the same stuff. Yep, ten years ago, the same today. It's recruitment, onboarding, it's unconscious bias training, assertiveness training, whatever the training programs are.' Yet there's been minimal change in outcomes during that period, he observed, and few clearly measurable processes. It's worth noting that despite these firms offering advice to clients on improving DEI outcomes, several had significant gender pay gaps when employer data was first published in 2024. Perhaps they need to apply a bit more scrutiny to their own processes.

The key attributes outlined as organisational 'leadership capabilities' can perpetuate masculine parameters. Leadership coach and former head of DEI (diversity, equity and inclusion) at Westpac, Jane Counsel, has often noted the trend when working with people who are being assessed against capability frameworks for development plans and performance assessment. Bias is ingrained in concepts of leadership, and the language used, she explains. When there is talk about business acumen, for example, there may be assumptions about required experience and tenure, which can negatively impact women who might have not had as much technical experience in a role, or have taken time out with caring.

As an example, Counsel mentions some commonly used criteria for executives, which include managing relationships, customer-facing capabilities, showing resilience and courage, and strategic thinking.

There's a number of those capabilities like, for example, strategic thinking, that people may automatically unconsciously and consciously assume that male leaders have greater expertise in. When it comes to customer skills, there'll be unconscious biases around things like managing relationships that might reinforce females as better suited to those roles. So I always say what sort of biases does the language still create, first and foremost, and trigger in people? Of course there are also organisations where capability frameworks are very immature or loosely referenced so there is greater tendency to default to our unconscious biases around what the typical (usually white and male) leader looks like.

Capability frameworks are an important part of the process of assessing an individual's readiness for a leadership role, development needs and so on – but it is really important that the process doesn't become just another way to reinforce systemic biases that continue to develop and promote a stereotypical leader at the expense of bringing greater diversity into the leadership team.

Some of the practical courses that open the door to influential positions such as board roles also continue to link suitability for authority with masculine qualities. The Victorian Gender Equality Commissioner, Dr Niki Vincent, told me a former colleague had done a directors' course in early 2023 and was dismayed at the tone of the teaching.

She was messaging me from the program saying:
'Oh my God, Niki, you wouldn't believe it, all the
examples are male and they use male as a default'
… She said they were talking about how they'd
make decisions about a board member, and the man
running the session asked, 'So would we take a
woman?' Everyone apparently looked on in shock.

The problem with gendered leadership models is so deeply
entrenched and self-reinforcing that even academics in top
business schools who are focusing on gender equity often
have little choice but to point out the anomalies at their own
institutions. HBS academic Boris Groysberg, and director
of the HBS Race, Gender & Equity Initiative Colleen
Ammerman, note that it's clear to them that 'educational
institutions such as our own have a role to play in mitigating
workplace inequalities'.

The stated mission of HBS is to educate leaders who
make a difference in the world. Business leadership
lacks diversity of all kinds, thereby constraining, we
would argue, the potential for its positive impact
on the world. Our Black women graduates are
systematically less likely than their peers … to see
someone who looks like them in senior management
and are most likely to say that their race and gender
created career obstacles.[3]

Women are still outnumbered by male classmates, making
up 43 per cent of the HBS class of 2021.[4] In Australia about
41 per cent of MBA students are women.[5] This is out of

step with other degrees such as law and medicine where the number of female students has steadily increased to over 50 per cent.

It's possible to rationalise this male leadership focus as just reflecting reality, with little impact on outcomes for women. But the evidence shows otherwise. The careers of female MBA graduates from HBS differed substantially from their male peers, and there was even more of a disparity between black women and white men, Groysberg and Ammerman found. A longitudinal alumni study found that female graduates 'are significantly less likely than men to be in supervisory roles, have profit-and-loss responsibility and be in top management positions'.[6] It's not just HBS graduates; a global study of 4000 MBAs offered at a range of institutions also found women experienced slower career advancement and less career satisfaction than their male counterparts. Male graduates of these courses were twice as likely to be CEOs or senior executives.[7]

Case studies focusing on successful business leaders are ubiquitous in many business school courses and bestselling leadership books, like Jim Collin's *Good to Great*. It's an approach associated with HBS that has been exported around the world. Many of these cases are written up by academics, published and used in management teaching. They set out details about how a business and its leadership have founded or built up the organisation, with a focus on steps to follow (or lessons learnt from failure). These have been dominated by white male leaders and a lack of female protagonists, Groysberg and Ammerman found.[8] Analysing HBS's MBA curriculum revealed that three-quarters of cases taught in the first year featured male leaders.[9]

The bias in case studies is common internationally: analysis of data from global clearing house, the Case Centre, found that just 11 per cent of bestselling and award-winning cases published between 2009 and 2015 included a female protagonist. Another study, of cases published by Ivey, the second-largest case publisher, found that only 10 per cent of cases published in a one-year period featured female protagonists. Even when they appear, women leaders can be marginalised. 'Analysis of student evaluations also revealed that cases with women protagonists received lower rankings from male students, and anecdotal feedback suggested cases highlighting accomplished women sometimes were viewed with scepticism.'[10]

The need to include women in case studies and leadership courses has been noted before. Research into the archives of the *Harvard Business Review* showed that there was a lot of discussion about women's leadership styles and whether women were changing the face of leadership in the late 1980s and early 1990s, Colleen Ammerman told me. Nevertheless, when you think of iconic leaders today, she said, they exhibit pretty traditional masculine traits, which we really still associate with leadership.

> I do think there's some progress that has been made in talking about how leadership should be different from the traditional command and control model, and how qualities that women tend to bring to bear are important to being an effective leader. That's the whole transactional versus transformational leadership notion, and research has demonstrated that women tend to be quite good at transformational leadership.

I think business schools have spent a lot of time talking about that, and at HBS certainly trying to evolve how we characterise leadership, in light of that more nuanced understanding.

Similar efforts were made to actively include gender and intersectionality in a review of leadership norms in Australia in the early 1990s, I'm reminded by Dr Jacquie Hutchinson, a former academic at University of Western Australia Business School. A taskforce was set up in 1995 by the Keating Labor government to look at the capacity of Australian leadership and management. Chaired by David Karpin, former CEO of Argyle Diamonds, it aimed to identify best practices worldwide and make recommendations as to how these could be applied in Australia.

The review called for investigations into identifying key leadership areas and development of curriculum. Despite that brief, the project overlooked the need for a focus on gender and/or diversity, so Hutchinson and two colleagues wrote to the review outlining this oversight. They then got a grant to look at gender, which resulted in the development of a unit for business schools and a book, and Edith Cowan academic Professor Catherine Smith wrote a paper 'Diversity awareness in management education'.[11]

Smith quoted leadership expert Alistair Mant, who advised the taskforce and noted that '"corporate Australia's Achilles' heel" was its all-male monoculture, whose "rugby-scrum mentality" made it difficult for women – and men who did not fit this particular image – to break in.' Mant said, 'Australian management culture needed to embrace a variety of differing perspectives'.

'The final report of the Task Force ... highlighted the strong inter-relationship between the highly gendered nature of both management education and management practice, whose inherent contradictions represented major impediments to more equitable participation of women in management', Smith noted.[12]

Although there was some impact from the findings, change in management gender norms and education has been slow in the 30 years since, says Hutchinson.

Given the continuing male bias woven through leadership teaching, siphoning women into their own leadership courses sounds like a solution. But it can sometimes add to the problems. Many of these programs are a sidebar to existing curriculum, which can frame women as needing special attention to make the grade. Course content may put the onus back on women to do the adapting. Plus these courses can only do so much to help with tactics, when the bias and sexism in workplaces haven't changed.

I should stress that this remedial approach to women is the core problem here, but not necessarily networks that support women by acknowledging and offering different ways of addressing sexism and barriers. But even support networks can only go so far if bias remains entrenched and based on stereotypes. This is a dynamic that Niki Vincent told me she has observed in some areas of government.

We have quite a number of programs for women considering standing in local government elections. I'm sure that they're helping women understand what is involved in being in local government, and encouraging them to apply. But the problem is when

they get into local government, there are all these
people on the council who haven't been through
any leadership programs, who behave like a pack of
animals and the women won't stay. So in spite of what
we're doing in those leadership programs, whether it's
fixing women or helping women apply to go into local
government and get elected, it's not working because
we're not fixing the other side of the equation.

Addressing toxic environments and traditional masculine
norms is well overdue, as Vincent points out. But it's interesting to note this hasn't deterred a growing group of women,
who see themselves as leaders and are joining programs
offering practical information on running campaigns and
entering politics (which I examine in Chapter 6).

The male bias in leadership models, training and higher
education is also reflected in popular leadership theories.
These tend to be cyclical, with a wave of interest in models
such as servant, transformational and authentic leadership
spreading before being replaced by another version. But one
part of these frameworks has been remarkably consistent;
they tend to have a strong adherence to a limited set of
individual characteristics, a reliance on heroic leaders, and
little attention or allowance made for gender, according to
Professor Terence Fitzsimmons of University of Queensland
Business School.

In a review of leadership theories, Fitzsimmons found
that the emphasis is usually on a traditionally powerful
gender and racial group, and this continues to prevent
access to corporate leadership for diverse individuals.[13] The
favoured leadership styles are also drawn from a narrow

band. A review of contemporary leadership research found only 5 per cent of articles related to the examination of participative or shared leadership, even though it is hypothesised that shared models of leadership dominated most of human history. In particular, researchers focus on heroic models of leadership, perhaps because these reflect male hierarchical ways of leading and dominate nearly every institutional setting researchers are likely to encounter.

Leadership approaches certainly haven't shifted a lot, said Fitzsimmons. The only specific gender focus in the current University of Queensland (UQ) MBA is a unit he teaches about gender inequality and gender in leadership, but that's because it was a priority for him and wouldn't be included otherwise. However, a recent review of the MBA program at UQ will see the specific inclusion of a unit on gender equality in leadership from 2025 onwards.

Although there has not been a great deal of attention on the gendering of our leadership theories, Fitszimmons told me: 'They are absolutely gendered, there is no doubt about it. They were written by men after interviewing men in America, and you don't see much outside of the US mainstream around corporate leaders being interviewed about what corporate leadership is all about.'

While popular leadership theories come in and out of fashion, there have been relatively few popular new contenders in recent years. There's some interest in authentic leadership and responsible leadership, and in major curriculum there's still a focus on transformational leadership, which is now 30 years old, Fitzsimmons explained. The lack of attention to gender with these approaches is problematic in a number of ways, not least the assumption that these models are as accessible and effective for women as they are for men. A fascinating example is authentic leadership, with research into what it means and how it works in organisations, highlighting some potential traps for women and marginalised groups.

Interest in the approach peaked around 20 years ago, but while there has been another burst of interest more recently, there's not a lot of clarity around what it means or how to 'become' authentic, Global Institute for Women's Leadership (GIWL) researcher Alexandra Fisher explained when we spoke. 'The original approach was a very trait-based understanding of individual authenticity. Now the more popular approach is that it's a state or an experience. But what's considered authentic is often based on the norms of the mainstream, which is usually a masculine framework.'[14]

As Fisher's co-author of the research, GIWL's Michelle Ryan, points out it's critical to ask, 'Who gets to be authentic? And whose responsibility is it to be authentic? You put that responsibility on women but then punish them for femininity – women who feel they have to bring in the cookies to work for example', she said. This means women are left feeling like they don't fit in, particularly in male-dominated environments with strongly masculine ideals and cultures. Your ability to be authentic has been found to be linked to power, Fisher says, so the more power you have within an organisation, the more autonomy you have, and the more 'authentic' you feel. There's another element of this popular leadership style that is potentially gendered, too.

Authenticity is usually talked about in a very positive, moral way. So that things which are morally good are more authentic, people feel more authentic when they're behaving in ways that are ethical. But then you think of people like Trump who just say whatever they want and people perceive him as very authentic. So I think there's this other side of authenticity about how much you can get away with, and still be perceived as authentic.

Given there's already extra pressure on women to be consistently 'better' or nicer than male peers, this aspect of authenticity could also set up more difficult expectations. On top of all these findings, research also shows that feeling out of sync with your workplace has an impact on women's job tenure and progress, Fisher says. So if it's tricky for women to fit into authentic leadership models, this can lead them to make critical decisions on whether they continue to stay or leave these environments.

There's another model that has captured attention in recent years: the vulnerable leader, popularised by influential US guru Brené Brown. She preaches the value of owning your story, speaking your truth and loving yourself in the search for empowerment. Urging women to be 'vulnerable' strikes me as particularly fraught in many workplaces where they are already marginalised and subject to bias. It's a message – just like the confidence mantra – that is profoundly gendered, with the main target white, middle-class women, according to UK researchers Shani Orgad and Rosalind Gill.[15]

Brown's 'immensely popular incitements to embrace vulnerability at work and their many iterations, for example in advice literature and the mediated appearances of successful women in the domain of work confessing to their impostor syndrome and vulnerabilities', actually teaches us that the best way to cope with insecurity and inequality is to reframe them as an opportunity for growth, Orgad and Gill concluded.

The reaction to a powerful white man who says he's vulnerable is likely to be very different – and more positive – than to a woman making the same claims. Even telling women to spurn perfectionism and the 'Wonder Woman' model and embrace their vulnerable side is a site of privilege. 'After all, in times of such sharp and divisive inequalities, insecurity, and precarity, very few individuals can afford to be seen to be weak, vulnerable, and lacking control and to deliberately refuse the confidence imperative.'[16]

When it comes to this more practical domain of what leadership ethos and behaviours are reinforced within organisations, the area of training and development, just like the capability frameworks examined earlier, has leant towards more male-aligned styles. As Fitzsimmons says, it's the current leadership cohort endorsing their own model of success. They have a vested interest in identifying those who look like themselves because that's what they think success looks like, he added. It's written about, for and by white men, and the West has dominated so these leadership norms become gospel.

The gap between this embedded leadership model and the reality of emerging leadership groups is ramping up pressure to broaden the parameters. In early 2022 I reported on a series of PriceWaterhouseCoopers conferences for senior managers (mostly 25–35 year old) in a resort near Sydney. The group was remarkably culturally diverse, which stands in stark contrast to the firm's partnership ranks. While the managing partner at the time, Tom Seymour, assured me this group was the 'future of the firm', there's quite a gulf to bridge for that to happen. My conversations with the participants left me feeling that many of these talented people will struggle to see that future if there isn't much faster progress. They have alternatives and will walk away from employers that don't start to offer jobs and pathways for them. It's a brain drain waiting to happen.

UTS and AGSM (Australian Graduate School of Management) tutor, and Women's Business and Politics in Colour founder, Kat Henaway, says the way the business schools are teaching in Australia is not keeping up with the times and is incredibly antiquated.

> I find that universities are regurgitating a lot of old rubbish because we have older white men holding onto their professorial positions and teaching the outdated business theories from the 1800s and 1900s. And it's embarrassing, so people going into business education in this country are being taught an old, old white man's view of how business works. What we know since the GFC is that everything has changed and it's the younger guys that have picked up new ways of doing things. However, these are not the ones teaching business theory.
>
> I know that because I was tutoring Indigenous business students for four years recently and I was looking at the literature and theory given to these students. I thought 'I cannot believe these kids are

being expected to look at this really old crap'. There are so many new business models now and I felt sorry for the Indigenous students so what I do is I show them the latest business theory.

One of the new approaches is to look at leadership from a total cultural perspective, Henaway says (more on this in Chapter 6). Instead of attempting to adapt to strong traditional mainstream norms, this leadership framework looks at cultural dissonance and how to bring your identity safely into workplaces. But Henaway is also wary of over-promising and under-delivering with leadership courses and training for women.

We have to be very realistic about this. These types of programs hype women up into thinking they can change their institution and we want to be very clear that we can give you these tools but don't for a minute assume that your managers and directors are going to endorse what you present. We have to remember that fundamentally, our institutions still have a very racially discriminatory lens and that's because of factors such as The White Australia policy from 1901 to 1973. So it will take decades of reprogramming and redesigning institutions to leave behind this very narrow way of thinking about how they should be run and managed.

There's some frustration from participants after attending programs she's helped deliver (including the NSW public service Aboriginal Career and Leadership Program, and the Emerging Indigenous Executive Leadership Program at

AGSM). They think they have the new tools and knowledge and they are now going to apply that to their institutions, she said. But we have to be realistic, particularly with women, to help them to understand how incredibly difficult it is to influence your institutions to become more culturally diverse or culturally safe.

A key focus of the programs Henaway has taught is giving women the tools to understand how to redesign strategy and also influence it, while also teaching them to do that in a safe way and through self-care. They will be coming up against the dominant regime, push back and a lot of disappointment, Henaway said. Many find that despite support from their immediate managers, there are more senior layers to negotiate in getting new ideas and approaches accepted.

Melbourne University senior lecturer in leadership Victor Sojo Monzon teaches leadership courses to under-graduates and he makes sure he shows them pictures of different kinds of leaders such as Donald Trump but also Hugo Chavez from Venezuela. This duo share some core characteristics: they are both very charismatic and really toxic people, even though they are from different sides of the political spectrum, he said. He also shows images of US senator Alexandria Ocasio-Cortez, Malala Yousafzai and the Dalai Lama.

> So I'm trying to show them different ethnic
> backgrounds, sexual orientation, gender identity
> and people with disability, so that they start to see
> that there are different people who could make it to
> leadership. But whether I like it or not, once they go

into contemporary workplaces in Australia, that is not exactly what they see. So there will be people who are teaching these students who are not really engaging in any kind of social critique, or the implications of thinking about leadership in this way. Or we use case studies to teach, let's say examples from Harvard Business Review, or any of these outlets that produce case studies from international business schools. While the last 10 years were better than the last 20 years, relatively speaking, there are very few cases dealing with just having women in positions of leadership.

The hunt for alternative models to study is tricky, Sojo Monzon added. The few black women in leadership, for example, tend to be in organisations such as the military. These limited examples also tend to be women who have succeeded through replicating very masculine attributes; their careers illustrate how women make it in a male-dominated work environment. The context of leadership is also very important, he explained, with leadership taught differently in undergraduate degrees to the way it is handled in a business school.

And so if you want to be a successful business leader, if you're doing research and business studies in management and finance and economics, because that's what you want to do, then that could colour the way that you're making interpretations … And if you don't have any extra motivation, to engage in a more critical approach to leadership, you simply won't do that. Even when I put that on the table for you to do.

It's also important to talk about backlash when tackling leadership behaviours and what are considered 'successful' qualities. Being assertive and extroverted could be considered stereotypically masculine, but if women show those behaviours they could be perceived as being domineering, over the top and too controlling, he said. He reminds students that context matters here because the same behaviours are seen by stakeholders differently depending on the person who exhibits them. If examples of diverse leaders are limited, it's another indicator the traditional criteria of 'successful' leadership urgently needs rethinking.

It's not just the the content of leadership courses that needs more diversity. Despite more women in management and academia, leadership role models and teachers in many formal programs and in business schools are still more likely to be male, said director of AGSM's general management program Matthew Byrne.

> We are so focused on evidence-based teaching we are 10 years behind the trends and rely on males to teach women how to lead. I insist on a 50 per cent male/female teaching split and my programs are all balanced that way. This is not supported or rewarded at universities, and I need to be quite dogmatic in maintaining this approach. I have had to walk away from great opportunities as I refused to run a program with all men teaching, when the stated objective is to increase female participation in our programs.

It's also essential that existing and new leadership theories apply a gender lens so their impact on women is taken into account. Fisher and her colleagues at GIWL, for example, are still examining the way organisations can tackle the gendered aspects of authenticity. While they haven't got the answers yet, they are finding 'that if you're going to choose who has to budge here – either women and marginalised individuals, or the environment and the organisations – we're saying that the organisations need to be doing the work to create that sense of fit rather than women having to do that work themselves'.

While the saturation of masculine mainstream models can seem impenetrable, there are other encouraging signs the cracks are showing. The fall of the heroic model is more likely as corporate collapses leave individual directors (particularly in countries like Australia) legally liable for the actions of autocratic types, according to Fitzsimmons. In fact, the alpha leader who is prone to hubris is now often considered a risk for the board.

There's certainly a long list of domineering or command-and-control style leaders in Australia and internationally who have come a cropper in recent years: former prime minister Scott Morrison; CEOs such as James Hardie's Jack Truong; Sony Music's former Australian head Denis Handlin; and former CPA CEO Alex Malley all eventually faced backlash for their styles and left their jobs. But as the unedifying prospect of a potential cage fight between Mark Zuckerberg and Elon Musk reminds us, the posturing of these leaders hasn't exactly faded away.

I've already mentioned the remarkably long rope and excuses for men with colourful personalities, such as former UK prime minister Boris Johnson and Tesla's Elon Musk. In fact, their erratic behaviour and bending of the truth is sometimes considered part of their appeal. On the other hand, there has been sustained criticism of the manner, effectiveness and personal decisions made by women leaders such as former prime minister Julia Gillard, who some critics even labelled the worst prime minister Australia had ever had despite passing a record amount of legislation; CEO of Team Global Express and former CEO of Australia Post Christine Holgate, who was lambasted for giving her executives luxury watches for a major deal that resuscitated the organisation; or in the US, the former CEO of Yahoo Melissa Mayer, who was criticised for bringing her children to the office.

These double standards, and the risks of alpha behaviour, are on the radar particularly for younger workers who expect leaders to look and behave differently. HBS's curriculum and case studies have become more diverse, and so has demand from an increasingly diverse group of students, according to Colleen Ammerman. But there's more work to be done in dismantling gendered leadership norms, she told me during an interview.

> I do think that has shifted, thinking about our own curriculum and culture at the school. But sometimes what we neglect is the other side of the equation, which is how we just talk about women in general, and our prescriptive gender stereotypes. So maybe we have made it OK, or tried to make it OK, for leaders to be, more 'feminine' or less 'masculine', but we still haven't really made it OK for women to be different from a prototypical [model].That's where it gets very tricky, and where you have that double bind.

Where women step out of the gender norm there can be harsh consequences in how they're perceived and treated. So we need to do both. Yes, let's talk about how to change our beliefs and stereotypes about leadership. But I fear sometime we're not as comfortable really interrogating our beliefs about who men and women are, or how they should behave.

Meanwhile HBS has been tracking the gender and race distribution of cases in the required curriculum, which had not been done systematically, says Ammerman. The school's required curriculum for all first-year students is being measured, and there has been some progress, with a larger proportion of those cases featuring women and people of colour. Some of the curricula changes to deal with these gaps, such as a required course on inclusion, were currently being reviewed when we spoke in late 2023. But demand for more attention to diversity in leadership teaching and examples was growing.

My initiative is actually working with the MBA program on some potential co-curricular programming, some discussion groups, for students that want to dig into topics of gender and other axes of inequality so there can be a space for that. And there's appetite for it. I've seen over the past decade increasing appetite, year over year, from students to learn about this stuff. And there's a real sense that this is important for us as future leaders, this is actually something that we need to know about. And I think that's quite encouraging as well.

There is also some welcome change in the lists of gurus and leadership experts compiled. Australian leadership expert Kirstin Ferguson has been featured in Thinkers 50, a list compiled by a London-based group, which includes a much more diverse range of people than more traditional lists. A dedicated gender focus is producing valuable work at a number of research bodies established within universities, such as the Australian Centre for Gender Equality and Inclusion @ Work at Sydney University, and of course the Global Institute for Women's Leadership at King's College in London and ANU. Many female academics I've quoted throughout this book are also working on research on the implications of gender on workplace, flexibility and leadership norms.

Board director and president of Chief Executive Women, Susan Lloyd-Hurwitz, says leadership lessons have been changing, although at a 'very glacial pace'. She sits on the board of European business school INSEAD, which has taken some recent significant steps towards a new framework.

> They have completely revamped their MBA
> curriculum to include sustainability in all the broadest
> forms and that includes gender as a compulsory
> component, not just a course, but within every course
> that they do. They have to have a sustainability lens
> on it … they are using the work that they do through
> the Hoffman Institute around the Sustainability
> Development Goals to inform their MBA curriculum
> … and have been quite brave … And it's not just
> around gender, but it is around acknowledging it's

about creating future leaders to make the world
a better place. It's not about creating the next
millionaires' factory or the next Goldman Sachs –
it's about creating leaders.

But there's an important caveat, says Lloyd-Hurwitz. When she was at INSEAD in 1993, the class was about 30 per cent women; there were still about 30 per cent women in the class in 2023, and the professors were overwhelmingly male. 'The gender distribution is still pretty much where it was when I was there in 1993', she said. That ratio may alter as the curriculum changes, and suggests business schools hoping to attract students in an increasingly competitive arena have a significant opportunity to boost intakes of women and diverse cohorts with a new offering.

A cohort of leadership thinkers, teachers and experts, despite often preaching the value of innovation and adapting to change, have continued to reinforce masculine role models and leadership styles. Thirty years since the Karpin report, popular leadership theories, business school case studies used around the world and capability frameworks are in need of an overhaul. Many are no longer fit for purpose, particularly as a new generation moves into the workplace.

The increasing female domination of management ranks across economies such as the US and Australia, and in sectors and professions such as medicine, law, pharmacy, veterinary science, and increasing collaborative leadership models in the start-up space, show there is no shortage of examples to draw from and profile. The academics I've interviewed were aware of this need to address gender bias and have been doing what they could to challenge it, which shows it's possible.

There's not only many female leaders, they have mostly had to forge a very different path and change the parameters of traditional boss jobs. They have a lot to offer because of, not despite, their gender. Women business leaders (many mentioned throughout this book) in Australia include Macquarie Bank's Shemara Wikramanayake; Team Global Express Christine Holgate; director Susan Lloyd-Hurwitz; AMP's Alexis George; director Miriam Silva; Koori Mail's Naomi Moran. And for starters internationally, Mary Barra at General Motors; Katie Bickerstaffe, co-CEO of Marks & Spencers; Amanda Blanc at Aviva; Ursula Burns, Xerox CEO; and JAL's Mitsuko Tottori are some contenders.

There are many valuable lessons to be learnt from the leadership of former world leaders like New Zealand's Jacinda Ardern, Australia's Julia Gillard, Chile's Michelle Bachelet, the Philippines Corazon Aquino, Indonesia's Megawati Sukarnoputri, Sri Lanka's Chandrika Bandaranaike Kumaratunga, and Liberia's Ellen Johnson Sirleaf. Women run multilateral organisations, such as Ngozi Okonjo-Iweala, the director-general of the World Trade Organization, and major financial bodies, like Christine Lagarde, president of the European Central Bank.

Have we got enough women in leadership? No. Have we got enough outstanding examples of women in charge of all kinds of organisations who can shake up moribund leadership lessons and case studies? Yes, we certainly do. Now we need to take them seriously and make sure the leadership canon is finally updated. But if knocking the great man ideal off its pedestal sounds like a big task in the short term, there are also plenty of ways to address the daily micro-aggressions undermining women's authority, as the next chapter examines.

Chapter 5
Addressing everyday sexism

A few years ago, I was a panellist for a forum discussing gender equity in financial services, along with three executives, including the CEO of a large financial employer. At one point, I started to respond to a comment by another speaker and got a few words out before the CEO waved his hands in front of my face and talked over me. In front of 200 slightly shocked women. I was so surprised I didn't respond – and have regretted this ever since.

Most women I know have been ignored or interrupted in meetings and know it's awkward to respond in the moment. I've learnt the hard way not to let everyday sexism go unaddressed. These days I grab any chance to make it clear that treating women with little respect, or bullying them to underline who's the boss, isn't OK. Age can make you more outspoken, and of course, I have more power than many women – I'm privileged and white.

Sometimes even the most fervent of us can find overthrowing the patriarchy is just too daunting on a busy day. But understanding micro-aggressions and then disrupting them can make a big difference, particularly when regular sexism is minimised or denied. In the face of escalating gender washing and backlash, taking steps to confront sexism at all levels is urgently needed.

The areas I've examined here tend to regularly turn up in conversations and anecdotes women have shared with me. They don't come with neat solutions, but I've also outlined tips I've gleaned on how to handle those awkward workplace moments, and how to have a constructive conversation about gender. And sometimes, it's not about doing more, but cutting back on popular trends that sound good but just don't deliver.

Band-Aid advice

Advice for women might be mostly well intentioned, but relentless lecturing of women about confidence and feeling like an imposter has over-promised and under-delivered.

It really took off during the last few decades of 'women's empowerment' or corporate feminism. A hallmark of this approach to workplace success is a focus on individual women learning how to be better – more confident, resilient, grateful and authentic (examined in Chapter 4).

I'm all for women's solidarity and supporting each other, but this stuff implies women need to adjust innate flaws to succeed – and it's their fault if they don't. I thought it was worrying in 2017 when I wrote *Stop Fixing Women* but it seems to have only grown since then. It's estimated 70 per cent of self-help books are bought by women and the sector is worth US$13 billion.[1] Individual confidence boosting as an answer to systemic sexism is everywhere, pushed by consultant, apps, podcasts, advisers and workshops as a handy way to tick a DEI (diversity, equity and inclusion) box. It's equally clear there's little evidence to show it's done much to mitigate sexism. If it was going to work, it would have by now: all those calls to lean in, lower your voice, remove the red lipstick and show your vulnerability should have delivered a drastic change in gender outcomes.

Of course, there's nothing wrong with advice per se. Nor with a pep talk now and then. We've all benefited from wise words and lessons learnt from experienced role models. I'm also regularly asked to give advice, so it would be hypocritical to urge women to ignore some of this wisdom, or just to listen to mine. But it's important not to confuse the symptoms of being less vocal in meetings, with the cause of the problem, such as power imbalances and male entitlement.

Lack of confidence is repeatedly used to explain away sexism by powerful men, I've noticed. I was told by a well-known man who has worked in senior roles in higher education that he was 'disappointed' by the failure to see more women advancing in universities. 'It's such a shame these smart women don't believe in themselves', he told me. Their deficiency was clearly the key culprit, not the way these smart, capable women were treated. Nor did it occur to him that blaming women was part of the problem.

Increasingly, women are noticing and challenging this glaring disconnect. A few years ago, I was invited to help judge some projects prepared by women involved in a mid-career leadership program. One of the groups decided to ask for feedback on the best advice for women at their particular stage by interviewing established business figures (men and women). The group couldn't help noticing that much of what they were told was basically contradictory. On the one hand, they heard women need to take risks, lean in, speak up and behave remarkably like an archetypal man. But at the same time, a few of the senior executives, mostly men, stressed the need for women to fit in, reflect the culture of the organisation, be a good team member and definitely not make men uncomfortable. And not to talk too much (more on this later).

The hackneyed idea that women need help with negotiating, lack confidence and are risk averse (detailed in Chapter 2) has been having a real renaissance since the pandemic, when men were front and centre as decision-makers. In 2018, Harvard academics Robin Ely and Catherine Tinsley reviewed the research on this trio of women-only inhibitors and found, after ploughing through meta-analyses of hundreds of studies, that there was virtually no evidence for these assumptions.[2] Whatever differences there were between men and women were so small as to be statistically insignificant.

Confidence advice is not benign because it masks the real causes of inequality, UK researchers Rosalind Gill and Shani Orgad have found.

> Whatever the problems or injustices faced by women or girls, the implied 'diagnosis' offered is often the same – she lacks confidence – to which the proffered solution is to promote female self-confidence. Inequality in the workplace? Women need to lean in and become more confident (check). Eating disorders and poor body image? Girls' confidence and Love Your Body programmes are the solution (check). Parenting problems? Just be a 'sorry-not-sorry' mum and raise confident kids (check). Sex life in a rut? Well, 'confidence is the new sexy!' (check).

What is striking is not only the similarity of the
discourses, programmes and interventions proposed
across diverse domains of social life but also the
way in which features of an unequal society are
systematically (re)framed by the confidence culture
as individual psychological problems, requiring us to
change women, not the world.[3]

There's another real downside to telling women to behave
in line with masculine norms. Research shows that 'when
women behave the same way in the office as men, their male
co-workers and supervisors are more likely to attach negative
adjectives to their behaviour. Those adjectives can make the
difference between a promotion and no promotion'.[4] The
same study also showed that women avoid backlash when
they adopt a more collaborative or administrative style of
leadership, rather than when they were overtly ambitious.
Urging women to just be confident needs to come with a
career warning.

The implicit idea that some stereotypical version of
confidence delivers the best results for everyone also needs
unpacking. If you think confidence workshops will solve
the lack of women in senior management, think again.
Australian economist and former chair of the Women in
Economics Network Leonora Risse used Australian survey
data to reveal there was no clear evidence that stronger
confidence enhanced job promotion prospects for women.[5]

On top of that, there is actually very little overlap
between confidence and competence, as management academic Tomas Chamorro-Premuzic points out. But the two
are easily confused when it comes to gender and leadership.

We (people in general) commonly misinterpret displays of confidence as a sign of competence, we are fooled into believing that men are better leaders than women. In other words, when it comes to leadership, the only advantage that men have over women … is the fact that manifestations of hubris – often masked as charisma or charm – are commonly mistaken for leadership potential, and that these occur much more frequently in men than in women.[6]

The effect of over-confidence on leadership appointments, however, is still tangible. 'Men are 34% more likely to be in top jobs at age 42' than women, and 11 per cent of that difference is attributed to over-confidence according to 2023 research.[7] But importantly, tackling this gender gap isn't about lecturing women to be more confident, according to researcher Dr Anna Adamecz-Völgyi from the University College, London, Centre for Longitudinal Studies.

Our results show that overconfidence matters, on average, for gender inequality in the labour market. But it is not the case that women are holding themselves back because they are underconfident. Instead, other factors related to the family, employment conditions and societal norms play a larger role in preventing women from entering top jobs. Improving gender equality in access to senior roles will require more than confidence building interventions.[8]

Confidence isn't the only unhelpful part of remedial advice for women. Some reassessment is also urgently needed on another favourite: imposter syndrome. This is an example of the mismatch between the male standards around leadership, and what is deemed appropriate for women, according to Professor Michelle Ryan. There's an expectation of over-confidence for men, therefore when women feel like imposters, it's because they don't behave that way. If you get treated like an imposter, then you'll behave like one, she says.

Calling this dynamic a 'syndrome' is an overreach, too. It's not a sickness and the term was first coined by researchers looking at high-achieving women who described it as a phenomenon, but it quickly became pathologised, as Reshma Saujani, the founder of Girls Who Code, sets out. The development of the idea that women particularly suffer this self-inflicted and crippling disease was no coincidence – it was a reaction to the surge of women entering the workforce, vying for jobs and gaining the right to control their fertility (now, of course, under threat in the US). At the moment, it's used to distract women from the real discrimination culprits.

> When as many as 82% of women report feeling impostor syndrome, it's pretty clear this is the result of structural inequality, not individual inadequacy. It's never really been about whether we're qualified enough, or smart enough, or prepared enough. Instead it's about the barriers that are designed to keep us out of those rooms in the first place.

It's leaders looking around and saying that the biggest problem facing women isn't paid family leave or pay gaps, a lack of childcare or a culture of misogyny; *the problem is us.*[9]

If you are ever in need of a feminist tonic, I recommend watching Saujani's 2023 Smith College commencement address on this topic.[10]

The effort spent on apparently benevolent but patronising advice for women is also about conforming to an ideal worker norm that reinforces a male primary-breadwinner model. It's in dire need of an overhaul because it doesn't reflect how women, or a lot of men, live and work. The lazy reliance on telling women to get their act together is also a reliable sign that gender discrimination is considered a female problem, and not a core organisational issue. This also leaves the power status quo intact.

The time spent on fixing women is an expensive distraction that hasn't done anything much to dismantle bias, while making a lot of women feel inadequate. My suggestion of a more effective investment would be replacing confidence building for women with workshops for all employees to address the pitfalls of hubris, autocratic behaviour and groupthink. There's lots of examples of why this kind of behavior, particularly during the Global Financial Crisis, resulted in disaster. This focus could also help challenge that dated ideal-worker model and encourage creating collaborative workspaces, where over-confidence is less likely to flourish and better decisions tend to be made.

Speaking out

Lack of confidence is often blamed for women's supposed reluctance to speak up or speak out as experts, but the reality is not so simple. As a journalist I've had a particular interest in seeing more female experts regularly featured in the media. Women make up just 30 per cent of sources and experts in Australian media reports (radio, TV, online) according to Women in Media's 2022 gender scorecard.[11] (WiM is a network of 6400 women working across the sector.) During the coverage and discussion about the results, it was clear that a key part of the problem was assumed to be women's reluctance to build a media profile.

My years as a reporter suggest women are sometimes cautious about taking a call from a journalist or stepping up to the podium. But it's often because they are targets for backlash when they put their head above the parapet, rather than a tendency to be shrinking violets. It also reflects the tricky standards women are still expected to meet. They are criticised for not putting their hand up and encouraged to speak out, but then have to navigate higher benchmarks and cope when they get viciously trolled about what they say and how they look.

At a workshop by the Women in Economics Network (WEN) on how to build a media profile (not how to be more confident), I got talking to one of the attendees. An economist at a well-known firm, she was happy to speak to the media, and often did. But she was battling a barrage of criticism from her male colleagues. They ridiculed her, and told her she was only getting the interviews because of her gender. She didn't need more confidence; the men she worked with needed to learn some respect.

The difficult standards of appearance, approachability, and 'acceptable' levels of gravitas apply to many women in the public eye. This bias is sometimes highlighted by men. A few years ago, Nine breakfast TV host Karl Stefanovic made a point of wearing the same blue suit for a year to see if his clothing would attract attention and criticism in the same way as the clothes of his co-host, Lisa Wilkinson. It didn't. 'I'm judged on my interviews, my appalling sense of humour – on how I do my job, basically. Whereas women are quite often judged on what they're wearing or how their hair is. Women, they wear the wrong colour and they get pulled up', he said.[12]

And yes, there is the paradox when it takes a man to effectively highlight the sexism facing so many women. His point was taken seriously, while chances are a woman wouldn't have had the same reception – or worse, she'd be accused of playing the 'gender card'. But making a concerted effort to challenge these contradictions can't lie on women's shoulders alone.

The support from WEN for women economists has paid off and there are many more commentators regularly quoted or on our screens these days. Australia has also done a reasonable job of highlighting a broader variety of voices of female scientists in the media, according to cancer researcher Professor Caroline Ford. There were some incredible science communicators and definitely more women quoted in news articles about science in recent years – from a range of backgrounds. 'I think we've got some incredible Indigenous scientists that are quite high profile. I can definitely confirm that there's this incredible crop of amazingly well-spoken women scientists that are more diverse and that are not all super senior. And that's been great to see, and I think that does go some way to inspiring other people.'

The notion that women are just generally more likely than men to avoid being quoted as experts has also been challenged in research by Associate Professor Kathryn Shine from Curtin University and colleagues from the Global Institute for Women's Leadership at ANU. They found a different story. The survey of 220 Australian adults who had given news interviews or who have the potential to do so, revealed that more than 80 per cent of people were willing to give news interviews. Women were just as willing as men.

The findings echo a study Shine did some years ago among 30 women academics that revealed 90 per cent were willing to pick up the phone to journalists. They were also reporting a mostly positive experience, with some caveats. Once again, the bias faced by women means they have to go about building their power and influence with more care than most men, Shine said.

> The key message, while recognising there are some key risks associated with it, is women do want a seat at that table and want to be given that opportunity and you can see why. So a lot of us in different roles are seeking media attention, and I get frustrated when I hear people say that women don't want to talk to the media or are much more difficult because that's not my experience. And certainly not what we are getting from the research either.[13]

Luckily, Shine says the message is starting to get through to not only individual women (the supply side) but has shifted demand from mainstream media. There has certainly been more recognition and awareness of the need for diversity across media. That's an opportunity for journalists to suggest using more women contacts and experts.

While there is much more work to be done, the ABC and BBC show that positive action is achievable by putting programs in place such as 50/50 The Equality Project, which works to ensure news and media content better reflects the communities it serves. Bloomberg has a special program to include diverse experts, and Shine has been interviewed for media organisation Al Jazeera on a program called *The Stream,* which aims for equal quoting of men and women.

> They say on every single topic they have found women to speak to them. Even on semi-automatic weapons … We just have to keep calling it out. Also, if we look at the big issues of our time then women are more affected by climate change, and make up many refugees, so how can we cover these stories and encourage governments to makes changes if we are not including those perspectives?

When it comes to changing the nature of who appears on our screens in positions of authority and as leading opinion formers, Shine says women are increasingly enthusiastic and gaining the experience they need. They don't lack confidence, but they do need opportunity.

Social media strategies

Navigating the difficult bind for women to blend being experts and modest (sometimes dubbed the 'modesty mandate') is quite a feat. Despite the progress reflected in Shine's research, the repercussions of this double standard and the backlash from colleagues has real implications.

Research from Australia's eSafetyOffice found that one in three Australian professional women experience online abuse in the course of their jobs; and one in four will reject job promotion opportunities that require them to be in the media or on social media.[14] Yet developing a profile on social media is an essential part of many jobs and helps build the profile needed for senior roles.

Even with these concerns, women are increasingly keen to contribute to social media as experts. Lots of the people surveyed by Shine said that while they had experienced trolling, they still speak to the media. They see the advantages of doing that and don't want the trolls to stop them.

Women in leadership are also using some platforms strategically. Women CEOs make up a much larger group of users, according to the 2022 'Digital reputation report', a study into the social media use of CEOs leading Australia's 200 largest listed organisations. The report found almost 85 per cent of ASX 200 chief executives were 'invisible' or inactive on LinkedIn, and just 6 per cent of all ASX 200 CEOs were 'very active'. However, women CEOs were six times more likely to be very active on LinkedIn; their activity generated four times more engagement than 'very active' male CEOs; and they were 3.5 times more active with posting than male CEOs.[15]

It seems women leaders are more likely to see the advantages of engaging with social media, despite the potential downside some may face on channels like X or Threads. CEOs like Telstra's Vicki Brady and AMP's Alexis George were particularly adept in using social media, the researchers noted.[16] The success of these efforts can also help inspire, normalise and amplify women leaders' voices.

Meetings, meetings

Who talks the most at meetings? Ask most women and you'll get a quick response: men. Ask if they've been interrupted in a work meeting and the response will usually be an eye roll. Time and again, data has consistently shown, women are interrupted and spoken over in meetings, and have their ideas ignored or appropriated, with some research showing men speak 75 per cent of the time in mixed gender meetings.[17] Addressing this takes some discipline and recognition of the problem, which can involve confronting denial or scoffing minimising ('Everyone gets interrupted, it's not just women').

Victorian Gender Equality Commissioner Niki Vincent told me she notices that even when the topic is women, it's men who are the first to put their hands up (which I noted in Chapter 2). They will often make a statement before they ask a question, then ask a question and then challenge the speaker about what they think, she adds. And they're completely lacking in self-awareness about it.

The syndrome is so well recognised it's been dubbed 'conversational manspreading' according to author Mary Ann Sieghart.[18] While men in authority often feel the right to talk more, she writes, it doesn't usually apply to women in those roles probably because of fear of backlash, and the need to balance saying enough to be seen as competent, but still warm.[19] In fact, data reveals that men and women speak about the same amount of words per day.

There's increasing evidence that putting the end to sexist behaviour in meetings and presentations would make a major difference to women's contributions (and credibility). Research has found that calling a woman 'emotional' or telling her to 'calm down' will make her point appear less credible to those around her and weaken her argument. My observation is it will also make most women very irritated. Meanwhile, men's credibility isn't negatively impacted if they're told the same things.

> People don't generally believe that men can be over
> emotional, whereas women have long been burdened
> with this sexist gender stereotype right back to
> the days of 'hysteria'. And these sustained biases
> genuinely have a massive impact on the world. In fact,
> a huge one in eight people still think women might be
> too emotional to work in politics ... Famously, [former
> UK prime minister] David Cameron attempted to
> weaken shadow Treasury secretary Angela Eagle's
> argument during Prime Minister's Questions in 2011
> by telling her to 'calm down, dear'.[20]

Patronising put-downs aren't the only problem when confronting bias in meeting dynamics – it's crucial to get more women around the table in the first place. But numbers don't shift behaviour unless the problem is addressed. US researchers Joan Williams and Sky Mihaylo suggest it's not enough to be aware of double standards, stereotyping, interruptions and taking credit for women's work. You have to do something about it.

Williams and Mihaylo recommend introducing a policy for interruptions rather than leaving it up to the boss to call it out. They even suggest keeping track of those who drown others out and talk with them privately about it, explaining that you think it's important to hear everyone's contributions.

> Similarly, when you see instances of 'bropriating' or 'whipeating' – that is, majority-group members taking or being given credit for ideas that women and people of color originally offered – call it out. We know two women on the board of directors of a public company who made a pact: When a man tried to claim one of their ideas, the other would say something like 'Yes, I liked Sandra's point, and I'm glad you did too.' Once they did this consistently, bropriating stopped.[21]

This technique is sometimes called amplification. Women overtly back each other, repeat an idea to make sure credit for a suggestion is given, or when a woman is interrupted that she gets a chance to finish her point.

Gender labour and Queen Bees

While double standards and bias are unfair enough, if women in authority acknowledge the challenges they face, or make a habit of promoting women, they can face accusations they are playing favourites. If they don't, they are tagged as nasty Queen Bees. The onus on women in authority to behave consistently as gender flag-bearers for all their sisters (dubbed 'gender labour'), as examined in Chapter 3, doesn't seem to apply to men. If a senior man turns up to a diversity event he often gets praised, but women leaders find they are often scrutinised and criticised for not doing enough to help other women or improve cultural diversity, for example. Giving a small cohort of senior women in an organisation responsibility for mentoring lots of women employees is a classic example. It's time-consuming, but not valued or rewarded. Loading women or senior executives from marginalised racial groups with the responsibility for addressing sexism and racism also leaves the problems in the special interest basket, which risks a lack of attention and action.

Meanwhile, the belief that power turns some women into 'ladder pullers' who fail to pay it forward for other women (not something men face) is mostly not backed by evidence. More women in top-tier jobs has a positive effect on promotions for other women, according to economics professor at University of Virginia Amalia Miller and her co-author, Norwegian School of Economics' Astrid Kunze.[22] Women in senior roles significantly improve women's promotion rates throughout an organisation. The presence of senior women, in studies of law and consulting firms, has also been found to decrease 'the likelihood of departure for their women subordinates: seeing women in leadership roles implies that career advancement is viable, thus encouraging junior women to remain', according to Groysberg and Ammerman.[23] And this effect is not just in elite white-collar professions, they point out, with women's job departures in the healthcare sector also influenced by their perception of the career opportunities inside and outside their organisation.

This link, it is worth noting, doesn't imply all women are supportive or indeed behave nicely to each other all the time. They don't. They're human, and just as flawed as the next man. But women are expected to be nicer and better than men, and savaged when they don't meet the brief (or object to gender equity steps due to the internalised misogyny described in Chapter 2). That's why we tend to remember the nasty woman boss but shrug when a man misbehaves. When I hear that a woman was 'the worst boss I ever had' or failed to stick up for other women, I usually respond that I've had male bosses who weren't impeccably behaved, nor defenders of other men. Expecting women to do all the messy gender work, and wave the flag for equity, with a saintly smile, is unfair and sexist.

Call me by my name

Australians have a particular habit of giving each other nicknames, usually a surname with a 'y' or 'o' added to the end: Thommo, Millsy, Jonesy. Or at least Australian men have this habit. Women are not as likely to earn these tags or give them to their colleagues. It's even apparent in popular culture: the hosts of some FM radio programs and breakfast TV shows combine a nickname for the male host (Jonesy) with the first name of the woman (Amanda), or Hughsey (man) and Kate; Shirvo (man) and Natalie. When it's two men hosting, on the other hand, they're more likely to both be known by nicknames, for example, Fitzy and Wippa.

What we call each other in workplaces can also be noticeably gendered. Public sector executive Adam Fennessy, now head of the Department of Agriculture, noticed the tendency for some men to use nicknames as a bonding tool, but rarely give the tags to women, so he did something about it. He asked employees in a service network that reported to him some years ago to use first names only for everyone. Despite grumbles, it soon became the norm.

There's also a huge reliance on the ubiquitous term 'mate' in Australian conversations. Although it has a charm to it, and is handy socially and in workplaces, it remains mostly part of bloke-speak. As a colleague once remarked, in the newsroom you could hear men ringing up contacts to see if they would be interviewed and liberally sprinkling the magic 'mate' word through the conversation to ease the process. Women don't generally use the term as often, or in this way, and would mostly not get the same response.

When it comes to younger female leaders in workplaces, on the other hand, research shows there's a tendency to give them generic pet names, or even assume they are students or support staff.[24] This can particularly apply to women from diverse cultural backgrounds, combining assumptions about their race with sexism. They may also face another set of problems with surnames, including those in contention for leadership positions.

Much has been written about the way bias shows up when recruiters sort applications according to gender and/ or ethnicity. Avoiding this has led to the use of anonymous recruitment, where names and educational institutions are redacted from applications. But while the research on this has often looked at bias in broad or entry-level recruitment, some of the same effect also occurs with leadership candidates.

There's pronounced discrimination against ethnic names in the recruitment of leadership positions, according to Professor Andreas Leibbrandt of Monash Business School. 'Ethnic minorities received 57.4 per cent fewer call-backs than applicants with English names for leadership positions.'[25] The findings are 'consistent with Implicit Leadership Theory where recruiters focus on an ideal or typical leader that is likely to be successful', he concluded. Bad luck if you happen to be a woman with an ethnic name applying for leadership jobs. The intersection of sexism and racism is a notoriously difficult mix to face. Organisations need to think carefully about steps to improve recruiting at all levels if they want to see different outcomes in leadership ranks.

There's also been lots of attention paid in recent years to the use of non-binary pronouns. The force of reaction to this shift has revealed these are not trivial matters, and something in the outrage from certain cohorts reminds me of how adopting the title 'Ms' instead of Mrs or Miss (which I've done for decades) continues to draw comment or even ridicule. I'm often asked outright why I choose to use the title. I try to be patient and respectful in my response. For those who identify as non-binary the choice is fundamental, as Kath Sciacca, who works at the Diversity Council, explains.

> No matter the journey you are on, when it comes
> to respecting people's pronouns, you don't need to
> understand it all to be respectful. I get that it might
> feel weird sharing your pronouns, however I like to

remind people that while it lets others know how to refer to you, the greater impact is that it helps to create a safer space for others to share, especially those that have faced situations where it is not safe to do so. It also helps to normalize using pronouns and removing the association and connection of them with gender expression. You really can't judge a book by its cover. Every individual has a story, and every individual has the right to express themselves as they wish.[26]

Language and particularly what we call each other reflects the norms in our relationships at home, in society and at work, and power dynamics. It's not a trivial matter. Formal titles, for example, the generic 'chairman', have been shown to reinforce the idea that leaders are male. Nicknames are sometimes affectionate, but you need to get approval from the recipient. Names are clearly about identity and tradition, too – just bring up the topic of women changing their names when they marry and watch the fireworks.

Old habits die hard, and even minor objections can spark backlash about political correctness. But framing it as an issue of safety and respect, and asking people how and what they'd like to be called is common sense. It does need to be on the agenda for anyone with authority, and not left for vulnerable or marginalised people to navigate.

Choose your words

The language of leadership is loaded with masculine sporting or military expressions. It's muscular, match fit, battle scarred, in the trenches, on even playing fields where home runs and goals are being kicked. Team coaching metaphors are pervasive, too, despite quite basic differences between a workplace and a football pitch. Good or bad team players seem to pop up alarmingly often in feedback, as though auditing or sales is just like a cricket match. I'm not much of a team sports fan. So when I first heard workmates talking about an 'own goal' or a 'slam dunk' I really didn't know what they meant. But it's a vernacular you need to learn to survive in many jobs (and very common in many workplaces). It will be interesting to see if the growth in women's professional sport and fan base will shift the gender connotations of sports metaphors in the future.

Along with sports lingo, military jargon has long been a source of amusement and irritation in the business world, points out London Business School Associate Professor Raina Brands. And it has a serious impact.

> The use of military parlance in organisations may reinforce historically rooted and implicitly held beliefs that business is no place for a woman. Military language helps perpetuate cultures of masculinity in organisations that by definition, exclude women. Jargon is a kind of linguistic shorthand that helps people streamline and co-ordinate how they work. But it also signals taken-for-granted beliefs and assumptions about who is included in decisions, has influence and decides the way things are done.[27]

If sports or war metaphors aren't your thing, then you might also find it hard to crack or even understand the banter that so often pops up in workplaces, particularly when the senior team is male dominated. Some Australians can almost lapse into another language with jargon and special lingo. Of course, objecting to this kind of communication makes you look like a massive spoilsport and the fun police – particularly if you are female. But sometimes the effect of this banter is far from casual.

While it can be used as a bit of informality and ease the workplace stress, it also acts as a kind of shorthand, and a way to help people feel included – or not. When women (or racially diverse groups) aren't taking part in the banter, they are being excluded from basic connections. Yet challenging these patterns can be fiercely resisted. I've noticed that those who are most often pulled up about switching to more inclusive language (or using gender-neutral terms) are often also the first to suggest that language is unimportant or doesn't mean much. Their annoyed reaction would certainly suggest otherwise.

In fact, there are many cohorts who find banter a pain in the neck or incomprehensible, according to a study by LinkedIn, which found younger workers wanted to reduce or get rid of it. Professionals surveyed said 'overuse of jargon can complicate communication and sabotage productivity', while '40% of workers say they've had a misunderstanding or made a mistake at work because they did not know the meaning of workplace jargon or misused it'.

> Many workers are left figuring out workplace jargon
> on their own, causing inequity in the workplace ...
> Professionals from non-English speaking households
> or English as a second language (ESL) are also most
> likely to say the process of learning workplace jargon

was stressful, slowed down productivity and made
them feel left out of conversations.[28]

No matter how they might try to fit in by using military
jargon, women will find they are running the risk of being
seen as aggressive, Brands points out. Because women are
expected to be warm and inclusive in how they communicate,
dropping a few military expressions into the conversation
could easily cause problems for them. Better for everyone if
less battlefield language is used in the first place.

The language used for feedback is also highly gendered –
particularly as women progress into management. Consultancy firm Textio provides tools to identify and remove
bias in language used in recruitment and feedback such as
performance reviews. It notes that employees getting high-
quality feedback earn more, and get promoted faster than
those who don't; and the groups who regularly get lower
quality feedback are the same cohorts consistently under-
represented in leadership.

Textio's research found that women are 11 times more
likely than men to report being described as 'abrasive' in
performance feedback.[29] The research also found patterns
of racial bias in job feedback: Asian men were seven times
more likely to have the words brilliant or genius in reports
than Latinx women. Likewise, US researchers discovered
that men received more positive words in their reviews and
women received more negative. Men were more likely to be
told they were analytical, competent and dependable, while
women were compassionate but also inept, temperamental
and indecisive.[30]

Paying attention to language and using tools to address the problem is a key step to dismantling bias in assessments and promotions. Both women and men react more negatively to criticism if it comes from a woman.[31] But the good news here is negative reactions were not so prevalent in younger workers, which could point to a generational shift. Some organisations are taking steps to address the problem, either giving feedback advice or alerting people to their biases plus using apps to 'debias' feedback and recruitment advertisements.

Finally, a word in defence of women's words and speech patterns. Oxford academic and linguist Deborah Cameron makes it clear that women's speech is often seen as a barrier for being taken seriously, despite its effectiveness and inclusivity. Women are often told to stop apologising, for example, although it can be an effective way of running conversations.

> In a male-dominated and sexist society we can
> expect women's voices, their words and what they
> know about the world to be underrepresented and
> undervalued. But if we want things to change, one
> important thing we need to do is acknowledge that
> they haven't changed as much as we've been led to
> believe by the standard progress narrative.[32]

Women face criticism for what they say, how they say it, for not saying enough or saying too much. Yet many successful women don't to appear to have read the memo about these deficiencies or style tips, and speak in ways that suit them.

As I've noted, women's authority is often questioned or ignored no matter how they talk, so breaking down boss bias and establishing wider parameters for leadership has to help shift these assumptions. In the meantime, while finding ways to disrupt gendered language, jargon, names and speaking patterns is not straightforward, some of these tips might help.

Micro-interventions: What do you mean by that?

Feminist author and advocate Jamila Rizvi has excellent advice when you hear a sexist remark in the workplace. Instead of uncomfortably letting it pass, she recommends turning to the offender and asking them 'Could you repeat that?' Even if they don't repeat it, the question shows the remark has been noted. Other circuit breakers to informal sexism and racism include asking 'What do you mean by that?' which puts the onus back on the instigator to either explain or brush off the query. Either way, the response makes it clear that the comment isn't OK, instead of letting it slide or an awkward silence descend.

I'm often asked what to say in those difficult moments (possibly in the lift or after a meeting) when a man asks a provocative question about gender – usually along the lines of how unfair it is these days when women get preferential treatment or are promoted over men with more merit. I've found asking 'Why do you say that?' or for an example or more specifics can be a way of shifting the power dynamic. Sometimes quoting a fact about what happens when there is significant progress can also help.

I've mentioned that some Australian workplaces have a tendency to use 'just joking' as a disguise for offensive comments. Comments that are racist or sexist or homophobic dressed up as 'humour' are still offensive and passive aggressive. A joke is something that everyone laughs at, as I once heard a kindergarten teacher explain to her class. It doesn't stigmatise, stereotype or belittle other people.

But it's awkward to rebut or respond to these cracks because you get told you don't have a sense of humour. For women this has a particular sting because they get tagged as nagging spoilsports, which further marginalises them. It's particularly difficult for racially diverse women to respond because they're already facing stereotypes about passivity, deference and humourlessness.

It's pretty embarrassing when a joke falls flat, so simply not laughing, and reminding your empathetic colleagues not to automatically go along with passive aggressive 'humour', can help. I've seen a senior man effectively shut down a 'just joking' comment by responding that it wasn't very funny. As most of us know, having a laugh is often the glue that bonds workmates together, as long as it's genuinely amusing and the humour is shared.

When it comes to tackling or going along with everyday sexism, such as comments or expectations that women 'play mother' and get the coffee, a friend of mine recommends asking yourself 'Would you say/ask that of a man?' It can be used directly too, of course. It's an effective way of identifying how minimising and gaslighting women makes them feel they are overreacting to innocent requests – and stops them from protesting.

Getting messaging right

Having a conversation about women, leadership and equity isn't getting any easier as over-optimism and gender-washing have gathered strength. For years I've been using a handy set of principles on framing gender equality produced by VicHealth.[33] The research on messaging and community engagement found Australians divide into supporters, opponents and the largest cohort, persuadables. This is the group that can shift from sitting on the fence to being active supporters of women.

Some of these tips on cutting through in conversations are counter-intuitive, and not the way I've often seen these discussions handled. For example, there's advice to talk about the core aim of equality for women and girls rather than trying to establish that gender equity works for everyone. Using specific examples of inequity rather than broad social outcomes (which many people think are about women's natural caring skills and 'choices') is recommended, plus a focus on men's advantage not women's disadvantage; and highlighting the solutions and positive results from tackling the problem.

Like many ideas outlined here, these are not foolproof. There's no formula to dissolve gender bias and take women seriously, sadly. But small interventions are surprisingly potent and they result in more than the sum of the parts. They can make a real difference, change workplace norms, shift gender expectations and, combined with the steps outlined in the next chapter, help more women get a seat – and a voice – at the decision-making table.

Chapter 6
Leading differently: Disrupting jobs, careers and power structures

Women might be missing from many formal power groups, but they have always been at the front of the barricades when it comes to world-changing social movements. Many of these trailblazers have been from marginalised groups: women like Indigenous rights campaigner Faith Bandler in Australia, and US activist Tarana Burke, Afghani Malala Yousafzai, and Swedish climate change activist Greta Thunberg.

Hearing Burke's story when she visited Australia in 2021 and outlined her decades of grassroots work for the most vulnerable women in the US, was a masterclass in activism. The woman who would become a global icon from establishing the phenomenon of #MeToo was also heavily involved in #BlackLivesMatter. A life of purpose, sure, and a brilliant example of leadership.

Standing at the helm of revolutionary movements that shatter norms, upset conventions and rewrite social codes is the hardest of all leadership jobs. It's usually unpaid or undervalued, like much of women's work, so many of these leaders aren't given credit for their extraordinary skills and media savvy. Their style of power, using solidarity and collaboration, is worlds away from masculine, command-and-control leadership that still permeates business and government.

But that gap is starting to close. Social movement leaders, particularly, inspire younger women, who told me they not only learn from seeing a different approach, but are motivated to tackle inequity in their own spheres. These high-profile exemplars also add momentum to the growing expectations, from voters, communities, employees and investors, for a shake-up in how leadership looks and who gets a chance to have a say.

Disrupting the old guard and creating a different version of success is a work in progress in most sectors. But as I examine here, there's growing pressure for wider pathways to the top in organisations and politics, removing a range of barriers, redesigning jobs with long hours, improving the way gender targets operate, and challenging the role of privilege. And some case studies I've included prove that leaders – including men in male-dominated spheres – can take immediate practical steps towards a different way of operating with major impact for women's access to leadership.

When membership group Chief Executive Women (CEW) launched a report on gender and race in leadership in mid-2023, a panel discussion between three leaders, Susan Lloyd-Hurwitz, CEW President; Shemara Wikramanayake, CEO Macquarie Group; and Tarun Gupta, CEO Stockland revealed the impact from not just prioritising racial and gender diversity but modelling it. There's no secret formula to attracting and retaining more diverse workforces, but the power of a CEO to set the standard is formidable.

At Macquarie, women make up 44 per cent of the workforce, and half of them are from culturally diverse backgrounds. After the panel discussion, I got chatting to a Sri Lankan Australian woman sitting next to me who works at Macquarie. She mentioned how different the environment was from other investment banks where she had worked. Diversity was normalised and your skills were seen, she said, which made progression much more likely than in her other jobs.

New power models

I discussed the impact from women leading social movements at a panel I moderated in 2023. Panellist, lawyer and Wiradjuri woman Kishaya Delaney explained that Indigenous women leaders were hugely important role models for her, including constitutional lawyer Professor Megan Davis and Indigenous leader Aunty Pat Anderson. Watching how they communicate, their knowledge and their commitment inspired her advocacy for the Voice referendum. But it's also about seeing how they operate and work as leaders within communities.

> It is amazing the way they speak. Having great mentors and having those honest and frank conversations about complexities – I feel like it gives you something to lean back on when trying to make an impact. Having someone who can advocate for you and learning from them how to have those difficult conversations and feel heard, it's learning those qualities. I don't know why we call them soft skills.

Those lessons apply well beyond Indigenous communities and translate into any context, including the top-tier law firm Herbert Smith Freehills, where Delaney works in the pro bono team.

Not too long after this conversation, I heard Indigenous woman Mi-kaisha Masella (mentioned in Chapter 1), a musician and student living and working in New York, explain how she's also motivated by female leaders to challenge power elites. At a 2023 discussion in Sydney on defining moments for women, she explained the impact of watching Aboriginal women like Faith Bandler and MP Linda Burney take pivotal roles in getting recognition for Indigenous women's rights. 'We're reshaping the narrative and we're kind of re-inserting ourselves – women and non-binary people – back into the narrative because we have always been here. We have always been at the forefront of these movements. We've always been the game changers, the people disrupting the status quo.'

Role models are still few and far between for younger Aboriginal women in Australia, particularly in popular culture, Masella says. An early defining moment for her was seeing someone who looked like her on television when (singer) Jessica Mauboy was on the TV show *Australian Idol*.

For me, it was so beautiful to see an Aboriginal woman so strongly and beautifully represent our culture … but I guess now, reflecting on my childhood, I'm realising that there's just so much further to go. I hope to be part of that change and I hope to make more space for female and non-binary people in all facets of the music industry. I want to

see First Nations women championed and given space
to be unapologetically Blak. I want my children to
grow up in a world and a community that encourages
them to speak their mind and stand up for what they
believe in – all the things I was told made me bossy
and opinionated as a young girl. Point is, I'm grateful
for the women who have gone before me and I cannot
wait to see new generations of trailblazers emerge and
add fuel to the fire that is Blak female excellence.

New paths to politics

The group of female independents who were elected in the
2022 Australian federal election upended many assumptions
about the political landscape. Their well-calibrated grassroots
campaigns were a surprise to many, particularly critics who
portrayed them as lucky to ride a wave of popular change.
Former prime minister John Howard even referred to them
as groupies because several received funding from founder
of Climate 200 group and political donor Simon Holmes à
Court. Their clever strategies cut through and were a stark
contrast to the complacent efforts of some more experienced
MPs.

There's a phenomenon in Australian politics known as
the 'good bloke syndrome', Holmes à Court explained at a
Sydney Writers' Festival discussion about the independents
in 2023. He described the way some male politicians
continue to rely on a knockabout and 'relatable' style, which
stands them in good stead for little effort, even when the
chips are down. He also noted that the lumping together
of these independent women MPs under the label 'Teals'

(a colour mix of conservative blue and environmental green) was never applied to the independent Senator David Pocock who also got funding from Climate 200. Would Pocock be a Teal, Holmes à Court asked, if he wore a dress?

When I mentioned this discussion to North Sydney independent MP Kylea Tink, she pointed out that the opposite of the good bloke is probably the 'nice woman'. That's not usually much of a compliment (or attractive to voters), we agreed. The nice woman is a bland, amenable and not particularly memorable figure. A good bloke doesn't have to be very competent, collegial or even actively pleasant, but can simply appear down-to-earth to great effect.

That's rarely the case for women. In her incisive book on male entitlement, Cornell philosopher and author Kate Manne outlined how different and exacting standards apply to successful women in politics, who have to earn their right to authority, and are expected to be not just highly competent but communal. In an interview with journalist Mahan Hasan, Manne explained what that involves.

> I think for women that's the condition under which highly competent women's power can become palatable. If she's perceived as highly oriented to caring, giving, serving others, and as attentive to every other individual in her jurisdiction. So obviously that has implications for politicians in as much as their power as women can be tolerated if they're both perceived as highly competent and extraordinarily caring.[1]

Just how anyone manages that feat of perception management, on top of a stressful politician's job, beats me. The Teals campaigned on some key issues: climate change, political integrity, and gender equity, which clearly resonated with their electorates. The motivation for standing in the first place was not to climb up a party hierarchy, and they had established careers before running for election.

The need to do more on shifting attitudes and the agenda on gender came home to Tink when she requested a meeting with Opposition leader Peter Dutton after winning her seat. It was fascinating, Tink told me in an interview, because he asked her about how her kids were faring since she got elected. She responded that it was a massive adjustment for them, but he would know that as a father.

> And he actually replied with something to the effect that, in his family, his wife took primary responsibility for raising their kids and that he didn't really know how someone who was trying to be a primary carer could work in politics. So it was really interesting, he was saying 'I don't know how people who have primary responsibility for their kids can be here'. And so, to me, that just opened a whole other window, as it hit me that's why our parental policies are crap. Because if you don't see yourself first and foremost as a parent, it's not that lens that you are considering the impacts of policy through. But here I am: a single mum who has pretty much worked my whole kids' lives, so for me, that intersection – that need for it all to work together – is unavoidable.

Conversations like this are a reminder that having more women in power arenas is essential for changing government priorities. Pundits predict there's likely to be more, not less, splintering of traditional voting patterns in Australia and other parts of the world. Giving female independents credit for their efforts and leadership, and the role they already play in parliament, could be a slower proposition. But they have already made a different version of leading viable and visible.

Expanding the pipeline

During the 2022 federal election, women from a range of different backgrounds stepped up to have a say in the national agenda when they got the chance. There's increasing recognition that the candidate catchment for many top roles has been far too homogenous and narrow – whether in politics, the public sector or business, and arts and community organisations. Broadening the path into politics didn't happen overnight or without concerted effort, such as targets and quotas and a major injection of effort from not-for-profit organisations founded by women.

Women for Election (WFE), launched in Australia by Jennifer Morris, and Pathways to Politics, founded by Carol Schwartz, provide women who see themselves as future political leaders with the practical information they need to run campaigns and get elected. The chair of WFE, lawyer and non-executive director Shirley Chowdhary, told me that of the 178 alumni who have run in local, state and federal elections since 2019, 46 have been elected (26 per cent), representing the ALP, Liberal Party, Greens, Animal Justice

Party, National Party, Reason Party and as Independents. This includes the first female mayor for the Torres Strait Shire Council. And importantly, hundreds of alumni have gone on to volunteer on other women's campaigns, an approach championed by former mayor and WFE partner Ruth McGowan.

The work of these organisations is an example of what happens when outcomes for women are a focus for philanthropy and the NFP arena. I've seen this firsthand as a member of the board of Australians Investing in Women (AIIW), which advises philanthropists on how to use a gender lens on their giving and programs. AIIW CEO Julie Reilly says the results from both these bodies demonstrate the tangible outcomes for women in leadership when there is gender-wise investing.

There's not as much progress in busting open the pathways in business, however. Eight out of 10 CEO pipeline roles are held by men, many with finance or engineering backgrounds, Chief Executive Women data shows.[2] The picture in the US and UK is similar. Only a few women have been appointed as the boss from senior female-dominated human resources, marketing and public relations roles, including Chanel's Leena Nair and Xerox's Anne Mulcahy, according to a report in the *Financial Times*.[3] But change is slowly happening, particularly as more HR heads are included in executive committees. There were also more women becoming divisional and regional CEO roles in US and UK companies, providing another pool of potential candidates.

The lack of women is not about a lack of experience, Denise Wilson, CEO of the FTSE Women Leaders Review, told the *Financial Times*. Part of the problem was bias in the selection process and perception of what a leader looks like, which feeds into the choice. But boosting the number of women CEOs must include a significant shift in recruitment practices: 'Either companies broaden their search beyond traditionally male-dominated jobs or step up efforts to appoint women to these positions'. Pressure to do this has been building. Some businesses have addressed the structural barriers by making sure women get broader experience, while there are examples of female board directors moving into CEO roles, too.

Across the economy there's more pressure for account-ability. The role of big investors – institutional wealth, sovereign wealth funds and big super – is putting a priority on investing in organisations that have a strong track record on gender, former chair of Aware Super, Sam Mostyn (before her appointment as Australia's Governor-General), told me. And increasingly they're looking down into the management of organisations, whether it's gender, or gender plus culture plus skill sets. She's seen a dramatic change in the focus on managing the risk and the complexity in the economy in the last few years. Companies now seriously have to respond by changing their way of thinking about the hiring practices onto boards and into management, and pathways for women.

But even with these parameters shifting, there are core challenges. The traditional expectations of executives working all hours creates the glass-hours ceiling, described in Chapter 2. Having the acceptable runway of experience remains difficult for many women. It can be many times harder for those from diverse groups. Kat Henaway, founder of Women's Business, which amplifies Indigenous women in leadership, has particular insight into the barriers facing her peers and women of colour in getting funding, sponsorship and networks to build their business or career – and to be seen as leaders.

As an adviser, Henaway has helped set up leadership programs for Indigenous and culturally diverse women, and says these formats tend to take a very different approach to the notion of leadership. The female trainers in this area are coming at leadership from a total cultural perspective, and they teach a new way of looking at leadership for a group that is so often marginalised and excluded from leadership roles. They are using some traditional theory on adaptive leadership, and around presentation skills, but starting these programs with training on identity and cultural leadership.

> What they are teaching women is around this idea
> of how you bring your whole self to work without
> having to minimise your opinion and views and
> having to 'code switch'. At the moment these women
> (participants) walk into an institution and have to
> switch their personality off from being a black woman
> or an Indian woman and have to pretend they're a
> mainstream woman. That means they can't bring all
> of their cultural knowledge and experience and apply
> that into an Australian workplace. What we teach is
> about 'don't leave your cultural identity at the door'.
> We've looked at this model and it works overseas.

A lot of incredibly smart women leaders, in what are considered to be less developed countries, are actually using the latest thinking about leadership, she adds.

Diversity specialist Julie Chai set up the Asian Leadership Project in 2017 with a clear aim – to dismantle the bamboo ceiling that many Asian Australians confront in the workplace. She was determined to get some serious attention focused on the incredibly low number of Asian Australians in senior roles throughout all kinds of organisations. Her experience as a Chinese Cambodian, Australian woman leader made her realise that the ceilings and challenges she hit were consistent irrespective of the industry or sector, she explained when we spoke.

> For me, it's always been culture before gender when it comes to my diversity identity … when I think about my three brothers, they do whatever they want. They had complete freedom to take risks with no consequences, but my sister and I were confined and expected to be quiet and compliant, to speak when spoken to. I've definitely seen an uptick in the number of younger Asian women that love the impact that I'm having on normalizing Asian female leadership because that, hopefully makes the pathway easier.

The Asian Leadership Project gives individual members the chance to network, join forums and attend coaching, but Chai also works with organisations to dismantle systemic barriers and bias. Most of the corporate members, ranging from law and professional services firms to banks, will typically have a cultural diversity strategy and programs such as internal mentoring programs, specific reverse mentoring programs, and events that are focused on sexism and racism. They're slowly moving the dial internally, says Chai, because they know the bamboo ceiling exists, and that they need to take action to address it.

Fine-tuning targets

As much of the evidence in this book shows, it's a pipe dream to think gender equity will naturally erupt across society without advocacy and concrete action. That's why I've always supported targets (usually voluntary) or quotas to ensure women are part of the mix at any level in any organisation. The Australian Labor Party's introduction of a quota for women against some stiff internal opposition has made a big difference to numbers: after the 2022 election, 47 per cent of MPs were women with 10 women in the Cabinet. In contrast, the Liberal National Party has long opposed quotas and struggles to boost the number of women in its ranks, with women making up just 20 per cent of the MPs in the lower house of federal parliament in mid-2023.[4]

However, with targets now used across many organisations, it's clear they are no panacea to gender inequity, given the slow progress at the top. Too often used as a 'set and forget' mechanism, targets often aren't well structured or don't get support from management, leading to backlash about unfairness. Critics also point out that they're often restricted to senior ranks and have little 'trickle down' effect for women throughout organisations.

I asked Professor Michelle Ryan about this dynamic. While visibility of women in senior ranks is important, she said relying on introducing targets, particularly at senior levels only, may not deliver sustainable change either.

That's not the only thing we can do. We have to have
quotas, but at all levels. We know that those women
who end up as minorities on boards often don't have
much power. So there's change at some dimensions
but that doesn't trickle through because there are just
not enough women in the system.

Former Telstra CEO David Thodey has made the same
point about getting more women into executive roles. It is
key to ensure targets are set throughout the organisation to
create a pipeline and not just at the top, he told me.[5]

Targets can work, however, if they are taken seriously
and not used to tick a compliance box. In fact, research
by University of South Australia's Professor Carol Kulik
on targets in Australia's public service found that it's too
easy to ignore, game the system or not properly introduce
targets.[6] When this happens, or there's the bare minimum
of compliance, the point of the target as a lever to inject
diversity gets detached or decoupled from the goal.

Integrated bundles of top-down (e.g. requiring
at least two women on shortlists) and bottom-up
practices (e.g. mentoring) can help avoid decoupling
by ensuring women are appointed to senior roles and
supported to progress through an organisation.

Chief Executives are key to ensuring a gender target
remains coupled with its implementation; Chief
Executives must provide visible support to internal
champions to make gender targets effective.[7]

The problem is the emphasis on bottom-up levers – offering mentoring, flexible work – has not created situations in organisations where women can support one another, Kulik added, because there are simply not enough of them at senior levels. Gender proportions in many settings really make a difference to contributions and outcomes (this applies to everyone – just watch the discomfort of a man who finds himself in a meeting or group dominated by women). When there are so many situations where there's one or at best two women on a board or in a leadership team, we haven't created enough of a critical mass to get any action taken, Kulik said. But when critical mass is there, it definitely does have an impact, she explained to me.

> Our data speaks very strongly to that. Maybe
> it's because there are just more women available
> in the system, or appointments maybe are made
> differently. But we also see that having women in
> senior roles, whether it's in the executive team or on
> boards, dramatically changes internal processes in
> organisations. We know those organisations adopt
> more employee participation practices. So there's
> more internal voice and more grassroots things going
> on. We know that there are smaller gender pay gaps,
> because the women just look at different data than
> the men do.

Top-down programs work faster, Kulik said, and getting enough women into senior roles will help get more women throughout the entire hierarchy.

The normalising effect when there are more than one or two women at the table is something CEW President and former CEO of Mirvac, Susan Lloyd-Hurwitz, saw firsthand. The Mirvac board has equal numbers of male and female directors, and the effect was apparent in a range of outcomes including the psychological experience for women, she told me.

> If you ask any of the female directors, what did it feel like being on the board compared to many of their other boards? They would say it felt normal. And I think this is a really important point: that their brain space wasn't taken up with thinking, 'How do I frame this? And how do I make my voice heard? When do I intervene?' It was normalised that half the room was female, it was a very strong signal that this was something that was very important to the board and that cascaded and went through the executive team. Mirvac is a construction development company with 40 per cent of its executives women, which I think is quite extraordinary for a highly masculinised segment.

Radical flexibility: Sharing boss jobs

The suggestion that more than one person can lead an organisation gets demolished by critics who say it just doesn't work. That is, until two people effectively do just that. The CEOs of Australian IT success story Atlassian, Mike Cannon-Brookes and Scott Farquhar, shared the job for 23 years, and the business has grown substantially and is valued at more than $50 billion (Farquhar stepped down from the role in 2024). Making decisions can be done collaboratively and on time. While there are only a few high-profile examples, they show that jobs with clout and leadership roles don't have to be filled by a sole heroic figure working ludicrous hours. Yet I've observed over decades of reporting on leadership roles that, if anything, there has been an intensifying of the extreme hours and sacrifices expected in many sectors. It's almost as though the price of entry to these powerful echelons is painful and total immersion, with no time for anything else.

This leads to a fundamental disconnect. It's between how women want to or need to work, with daily and career flexibility to manage a full set of responsibilities, and a very defined model of what senior roles are, and the 60-hours-a-week regime, Mary Wooldridge, the director of the Workplace Gender Equality Agency, told me in an interview.

> The more you can redefine the nature of those senior roles, to build in flexibility and capacity so that more women can both see themselves in that role and can consider putting themselves forward for consideration, the more that will break that dynamic. And job sharing is another example of that, in terms of how it can be done.

Despite a lack of attention and some scepticism, job sharing is a model that can work at many levels, including senior roles. Victorian Gender Equality Commissioner Dr Niki Vincent recalls demanding a different kind of job structure at an early stage of her career – and continues to put into practice.

It's the idea of radical flexibility, such as job sharing, and absolutely trusting people to work when they can work as opposed to the expectations that they're going to be available these certain times. I've always had it in every organisation because it was something I got when I first started work out of uni. I first met one of my best friends in the library at a university when we were both finishing study and applying for the same job. I had four kids, she was finishing honours, she said, 'I really don't want a full-time job' and I said, 'Well, neither do I, and maybe we could job share'. We went for it as a job share in 1994 and we didn't even know that wasn't a thing. We got it.

After that I expected flexibility for myself because I had four kids, and I wouldn't go if I couldn't get it. And then for every organisation that I've led, that's always been the way it's been. And I found I've had fabulous women working for me who couldn't get jobs anywhere else because they were breastfeeding or whatever. And I'm saying, 'Come and give me what time you've got'.

Job sharing has allowed financial services executives Catherine van der Veen and Lucy Foster to work in tandem for many years. Although van der Veen was very used to having complete autonomy over her work, it became apparent that working with a different way of making decisions was liberating.

So decision-making is what we're paid for in these senior roles. And the job share has taught me that if you're … very clear about what you're aiming for, there are multiple pathways to get there. Lucy and I have been very good at debating, and then very often we'll make the same decision. But then there have been times Lucy's made a decision that I wouldn't have, but I have enough trust in her, and then we both reserve the right to change our mind. It's complementary diversity between us, which we always argue is our signature strength.

Far from limiting their careers, after working at Commonwealth Bank Australia for a few years, the pair were approached to take on a senior job running life insurance company Generation Life. It was the first job-share CEO position that the women were aware of in financial services. The small, listed, life insurance company employed 50 people, but the role involved dealing with regulatory bodies, shareholders, staff and 10 000 customers at the time, so it was great experience.

Eventually the two went as a partnership to a senior role at financial firm Allianz Retire Plus. They divide up the role but have one set of accountability goals. It's practical because as van der Veen points out, a CEO needs to be a great people person, highly commercial, have a handle over risk, and a lot of personal energy for their staff. To find that in one person is difficult, but it's much easier with two. It can also make these roles seem far more accessible to women.

Some of the arrangements are not exactly rocket science but require practical reorganisation (they even have a joint

CV). Interest in job sharing is growing, although so far, van der Veen says she's not aware of any men job sharing at executive level in financial services. But she expects to see more examples, particularly following the increase in demand for flexibility since COVID. Catherine is currently helping two senior job-share partnerships at ING and OzHarvest with some of the learnings from her eight years of working in partnership with Lucy.

> The next generation of people coming through, I have observed, want to be more present with their family. That is absolutely a given. They want to study again, so a lot are taking sideways moves by having these portfolio careers. Others have aging parents, others just don't want to put all their eggs in one basket. They want to have a balance, they want to look after their health. They've seen what their parents have gone through. They don't want that for themselves.

Spending and risking privilege

Anyone with some power and privilege can play a role in changing the dynamics of who gets ahead – and who doesn't. I've mentioned how more acknowledgement is long overdue of the tail winds and the 'glass cushion' that gives men from privileged groups an advantage, and less scrutiny or penalties for failing, rather than focusing attention on women's assumed lack of confidence. This isn't easy stuff, as analysis of backlash has highlighted.

Women with privilege need to be part of beating leadership bias, too. Talking about gender equity in a truly inclusive way for all women is on the agenda and overdue. University of Technology Sydney academic and former Diversity Council Australia CEO Nareen Young says there's been a welcome change in the way advocacy for women is framed, and she is loving seeing intersectionality discussed, including social class, which she thinks is particularly important. But she also says there's a whole lot of work to do to make up the ground that was lost during a period where the women-on-boards discussion solely focused on upper middle-class white women and set the debate and progress back.

There are uncomfortable conversations that need to happen around the gender and privilege issue and what can help to address the problem, says Laura Innes, former deputy chair of gender equity group The 100% Project, and Coles finance manager. It's clear people don't like to be called out on their privilege today, she explained to me. Most of us would probably want to feel that we got there on merit, so for someone to maybe say 'Why don't we look at this with a different lens?' is confronting. But as she points out, drawing attention to privilege is not an accusation, it's about asking everyone to be more aware of those issues and their impact.

It might be awkward, but these conversations can make a big difference. DEI expert Dr Michelle King believes many of us can 'spend our privilege' by investing our time, effort and social status to support the inclusion, development and advancement of minority groups at work. This also means being willing to risk your advantages – to give up some of your reputation, acceptance and standing at work to advocate for others. Her suggestions include making an effort to understand what others go through at work; asking people from minority groups to share their experience; pointing out where some people run into problems with leadership and success norms; and making those problems visible. 'Spending your privilege is an intentional practice that aims to disrupt the status quo. This is not something you do once; it is an ongoing commitment to put equality into practice every day at work.'[8]

There has been growing awareness of the need for intentional efforts to ensure that gender diversity isn't only about women from the mainstream. At Coles, Innes says there are structures like a diversity steering committee, but they were also looking from the grassroots and up, and ensuring a range of different voices were heard. The assumption that fixing the gender equity gap would automatically resolve other forms of marginalisation has turned out to be overly optimistic. In fact, what often happens, Innes says, is replacing white men with white women, and the voices and interests of marginalised women haven't been included.

As a number of female leaders of anti-racism movements in the US have noted, the job of educating and ensuring resistance and privilege is addressed in workplace DEI programs is often delivered by white women. Decentring whiteness in these areas is a key step to effectiveness, and a reminder of the way intersectionality works to stymie marginalised groups.[9]

A case in point: Fixing the gender gap

There are not enough success stories of organisations really making big sustained changes, academic Carol Kulik told me when we discussed her gender equity research. I second that: a guiding principle for my journalism and advocacy over decades has always been, when possible, to show what can be done and offer examples. But there needs to be much more of it.

These case studies show how traditional male-dominated sectors can break down myths and do things differently so women can move into senior jobs and non-traditional roles – with better pay and progression. It's not only possible to boost women's participation; it delivers better workplaces and strong results.

Mirvac

The president of Chief Executive Women and former CEO of construction company Mirvac, Susan Lloyd-Hurwitz, says she's a massive introvert. But once she starts explaining to me the importance of creating gender equity at work, there's an animation and energy that takes her well into extrovert territory. At the helm of a listed company, Lloyd-Hurwitz invested plenty of time on getting practices sorted to ensure the male-dominated workplace was attracting and retaining female employees. It didn't happen overnight.

> It was 10 years' worth of hard work. We focused on
> multiple fronts at the same time because there's no
> one simple formula to addressing it. So a whole suite
> of things happened … when we started talking about
> the gender pay gap, people say, 'No one would ever
> do that. No one would ever pay women less,' because
> nobody sets out to pay women less. So the only way

to get to that is to shine a light on the data. So we said, 'Well, let's look at the data. Oh my goodness, yes, there is a gender pay gap'. And we fixed it immediately, on the spot, visibly, and it had a huge effect on the business because we were giving women pay rises who were on parental leave … And so the signal of all of that was just huge.

This was no 'set and forget' solution either. It had to be consistent because the pay gap tends to creep back in otherwise, she explains. The other area for attention was performance reviews, bonuses and pay rises. Again, robust analysis included gender distribution, performance ratings, bonus allocations and pay increases. This was not just at senior levels but also gave attention to the lowest paid employees, because that was a highly feminised part of the workforce.

Another focus was on retention of women, particularly around child-bearing stages. This included very generous parental leave provisions for men and women. The whole problem doesn't get fixed unless the participation in the workforce and in care has been shared equally, Lloyd-Hurwitz says. The company had close to a 100 per cent return rate from parental leave.

Equally, the pipeline of women was mapped out, and if there were shortfalls, steps were taken to find out why and then recruit to fill gaps. In fact, when she was told there were no female engineers to employ, Lloyd-Hurwitz told her recruiters to look in the mining industry or somewhere else. If recruiters provided a shortlist with less than 50 per cent women, they were told to try again. The same criteria applied to any bank or service provider that came to pitch and brought in an all-male team, she adds. 'We sent them away and said, 'No, come back when you've got a team that includes some women on it, please'.

Mirvac has increased the number of women in the workplace to about 40 per cent across the organisation and in management roles. It has also delivered healthy profits over the last few years and been recognised for its gender efforts, ranking first out of 4000 companies in Equileap's *Gender Equality Global Report & Ranking* two years in a row, 2022 and 2023.

ASTRO 3D

Science is generally better known for the enormous challenges than success stories in attracting and keeping women in the sector. The story of Australia's ASTRO 3D reaching 50 per cent women in its ranks in just five years, with a series of well-researched steps, shows if there's a will – and a committed leader at the helm – there's a way.

Professor Lisa Kewley, the founding director of ASTRO 3D (the Australian Research Council Centre for All Sky Astrophysics in 3 Dimensions) is now leading the Center for Astrophysics, Harvard & Smithsonian. She explained that a combination of sociology and psychology research was used to develop evidence-based strategies, and create a supportive and positive culture at ASTRO 3D to help boost female employees.

'Women make up just 30 to 35 per cent of PhD astronomy students, and less than 20 per cent at the highest professorial level.'[10] Professor Kewley was determined to do better, and that's what happened: ASTRO 3D's five-year program from 2018 to early 2023 increased the number of women from 38 per cent to 50 per cent.

The key steps included setting diversity targets with regular monitoring of progress; selecting a diverse set of team leaders; diversity training for all organisation members; ensuring 50 per cent women on postdoctoral selection committees and on postdoctoral shortlists.

It's a success story that can be translated to other organisations, the current director of ASTRO 3D, Professor Emma Ryan-Weber, has pointed out. Importantly, the increase in women running teams is setting up role models for younger generations, not just in astronomy but across the physical sciences and a range of technical industries, such as data science.

A couple of features proved particularly positive: when women ran teams, they recruited and attracted more female postdoctoral researchers, female students, and worked with more female collaborators. Once ASTRO 3D reached 40 per cent female supervisors, mentors and role models for students, it proved a tipping point. 'After that, student enrolments by women in the Centre accelerated. The gains were not made at the expense of men, as the membership grew over this period,' Professor Kewley said.[11]

The program continues to develop ongoing leadership development, promotion of work–life balance, partner recruitment, as well as pathways for reporting misconduct. Retention of women has improved at all levels. Now Professor Ryan-Weber hopes others will use the approach as a template for delivering better gender diversity in research centres. The story has attracted feedback from across the broader sector, including Professor Lisa Harvey-Smith, Australia's Women in STEM Ambassador: 'It just goes to show how quickly progress can be made when workplace change initiatives are properly designed, monitored, and evaluated'.[12]

Viva Energy

Jobs in an oil refinery don't top many job seekers' wish lists these days. Usually the opposite, in fact. So Viva Energy boss Scott Wyatt has to try harder to get employees for the business, which runs the Geelong Oil Refinery and retails Shell fuels in Australia. Facing climate change and an energy transition means the organisation has a big challenge in repositioning itself to attract people, he explained to me in mid-2023, because otherwise, they will end up with a very old male workforce – which is dwindling.

Truck driving is the perfect example, he says. Very few women are working in that part of the business, and the average age of the men delivering fuel to service stations is 56 years (and getting older). At some point, you've got no one to drive your vehicles and that day is not that far off, he adds. Then there are frontline operations, working in the refinery, refuelling aircraft or working in the storage terminals, which usually involves shift work.

These are roles that are designed to support, attract and reward men. So Viva Energy had to rethink the types of people that had typically done those jobs, and then redesign them and the paths into them to widen the catchment. Instead of trying to find people with specific experience or trade skills (women make up just 3 per cent of plumbers, electricians and other trades), the company opted to train recruits, and changed the protocols around lifting and driving heavy vehicles, Wyatt says, with rapid impact.

> It has changed quite quickly. We've gone from
> low single digits in the refinery to 25 per cent.
> So it's material, and critical mass. We've gone from
> 2 per cent to 12 per cent aircraft fuellers around
> the country ... it's made a change actually quite
> quickly. That includes behaviour, with more respect
> in the way employees communicate. The pay gap
> has also reduced to around 9 per cent.

The shift to attract women has long-term implications for the kinds of people who end up in management, too. Appointing executives for particular roles is an easier call, because Wyatt can make those decisions himself. But building a diverse group of frontline workers is much harder – and so important for creating the pipeline for middle managers, an area where the company has been quite weak in boosting diversity. The changes made at entry level will help to change that longer term, he adds, and show the importance of working on gender equity from the top down and bottom up.

His own motivation for focusing on gender diversity is the impact of pay equity and the implications that has on women's lifetime earnings, their subsequent dependency on the men in their lives, and ultimately how it contributes to a big power gap.

And of course you start with the fact women are taking home less not because they're getting paid less for the same job … but it's because a lot of the high paid jobs are designed around men … And then of course, you've got that definition of what good performance looks like: how people progress in their careers, the biases that comes from breaks in careers to care for families, and all that compounds, ultimately to deliver the outcome we have.

It's clear that Wyatt has a strong personal conviction that change is needed and he is a member of the Champions of Change Coalition (a group of 250 CEOs committed to achieve gender equality and increase women in leadership). But he points out that the influence you can have isn't confined to inside the organisation. Viva Energy relies heavily on contractors and suppliers and can make choices about who to work with, depending on their gender equity credentials. That's important as more women move into different roles at Viva, and may be dealing with other workforces that are still heavily male dominated.

That's often where you get a bit of conflict because the behaviours in those workplaces is not where it should be. So raising that with the CEOs of their (suppliers) organisations, and going, 'Hey, this is not a good experience, and what are you doing?' That's a good conversation to have.

Progress in some organisations is slow, Wyatt agrees, but the influx of women and their rise into management and impact as role models make him believe change can happen quite quickly if there is a commitment.

Australian Constructors Association

Sometimes practical examples that improve outcomes for women come from unexpected places. The Australian Constructors Association (ACA) represents one of the most male-dominated sectors in the economy, so its relatively rapid progress to 50 per cent women in recent years is all the more surprising.

According to several members, the idea came up during a dinner following a board meeting of the 18 blokes (mostly CEOs) who make up the ACA directors. Multiplex CEO John Flecker remembers it was a suggestion that quickly turned into a plan. It was partly born out of frustration that endless talk about improving the gender composition of the workforce hadn't delivered much change. Why don't we get every director to appoint a senior woman as a co-director? someone asked. There were few obstacles, so the ACA started to make it work.

ACA member and CEO of John Holland, Joe Barr, also saw the logic of the move. Along with other ACA members, he's been on a quest to make the industry more sustainable, and more diverse. Before this step, the ACA looked pale, stale and male, but once the membership changed so did the conversations. It became an accelerator for more action by company members and the board, Barr said.

The change didn't double the meeting size because the co-directors took it in turns to attend, and whoever was at the table had full authority to make decisions for their organisation. A couple of factors soon emerged. Many of the senior women were not engineers, and they brought different expertise to the table, so the focus of discussions changed to look more at people and governance issues, which shifted the dynamics, Flecker said.

> But on any topic, I think because we went to the trouble of diversifying, broadening the room, there wasn't much point doing that without seeking opinions from the people we invited in. And I do think that we've done a pretty good job of trying to seek opinions from the women in the room and maybe those who are new to the room … [they were] coming to a room full of all the CEOs and maybe not wanting to speak out too much, but they were encouraged, we said, 'We want to hear your view. That's why you're here'.

The current president of the ACA, Annabel Crookes, Director – Legal, Risk and Delivery at Laing O'Rourke, was one of the first women to be appointed to the board. Women currently make up 12 per cent of the construction workforce, a 5 per cent decrease since 2006, and less than 2 per cent of on-site roles, she tells me. But with structured action, some companies have turned around their results. Her own employer has increased overall female participation in the past four years from 26 per cent to 36 per cent. It has gender targets in its sustainability strategy, and in 2012 introduced an equal parental policy for six months' paid leave.

John Holland has also introduced a number of measures with feedback from female employees, leading Barr to concentrate on three areas: return to work programs; closing the gender pay gap; and tackling bias in progression. The company has introduced an 18-week, paid paternity leave policy for men and extended leave for women, and is working on more flexibility, such as using a roster system, particularly on operational jobs and project sites, where long hours are the norm.

One of the ACA initiatives is the Construction Industry Culture Task Force aimed at improving the conditions across the industry, including the pressure from typical hard dollar, fixed lump-sum contracts through to reducing the six-day week, Barr says.

> Through the cultural taskforce, we have five projects
> that are trialling a five-day week, and one of those
> jobs, for example, is the Royal Children's Hospital job
> that we're doing in Sydney and that job happens to be
> led by a very capable project manager who is female ...
> So as you can imagine, it makes a massive difference.

There's more work to be done getting women into senior operational roles, Barr says, and that's a dilemma across the sector. Many of the ACA members didn't even have a woman that they could appoint because they had absolutely none in the C suite, Annabel Crookes recalls.

> It caused them to really think about promoting
> women to those roles and making sure that they had
> the opportunity to turn up at that table ... but it really
> did start to change the conversation. And that wasn't
> just because it's men and women, but it meant the
> cognitive diversity was so much greater because you

had lawyers, not just engineers, and HR, professional strategy, accountants.

The impact of the board change has been tangible. The ACA has funded the Culture Task Force, and has also pledged that by 2028, 75 per cent of members would be Workplace Gender Equality Agency employers of choice, up from just two in 2023, and to encourage more women into the industry. Taking that kind of lead was simply not something that was at all likely just five years ago, Crookes said.

The members may be business rivals, but they clearly see the advantage of sharing intelligence on what works, Flecker said. 'This is something we all see that we need to do. And even for the greatest cynics in the room, and there aren't many … they say well, regardless, if we're making it better for women to be in the industry it is going to be better for everyone.'

The ACA revamp is a clear example for business of what can happen when there's a will to change the status quo. It was also the result of the efforts by some brave women who kept the pressure on leaders, and there's no reason more industry bodies couldn't do the same thing, Flecker adds. But would it work within businesses, too? It's a question that's been in the back of his mind. When it comes to some public companies, that's probably a little bit harder to do, he explains, with executive teams such as Multiplex's including regional leaders, so adding a co-director who is not in that role but gets an equal vote on something that affects the shareholders might present problems. But it's worth thinking about, he says – and maybe that's the next threshold.

Chapter 7

Elevating decisive women

The sound of nearly 6000 people, mostly women, loudly cheering as they got to their feet in a Sydney venue in 2022 was deafening. It was the tenth anniversary of former prime minister Julia Gillard's famous misogyny speech to parliament in 2012, and there wasn't a spare seat. Quite a few members of the audience were in primary school when those words ricocheted around the world, but they were applauding just as enthusiastically in recognition of that pivotal moment. With the benefit of hindsight, it seems that speech was almost inevitable, but it was a big risk at a toxic time, with plenty at stake.

I've heard many women talk about a series of crucial decisions they have made, personally and professionally, often against the odds and under duress. It's the best myth-buster around when it comes to the fiction that women crumble under pressure, can't cope with tough calls, avoid risk and lack the decisiveness needed for leadership. Given the urgent need to challenge boss bias and the delusion that women are given the same opportunities to become leaders, I was particularly interested in asking some remarkable women a core question: how and why had they made some big decisions in their lives?

Deciding to take your own path

Female trailblazers have always made big calls despite taboos. Australia's former Sex Discrimination Commissioner Kate Jenkins once told me she finds the saying 'You can't be what you can't see' a bit misleading. Women have frequently decided to forge into new territory, she said: becoming the first woman to qualify as a surgeon, become an astronaut, or win a Nobel Prize, for example. They couldn't see anyone like them up on the stage, but they went ahead anyway.

Economist Claudia Goldin, whose work on women and labour markets was awarded a Nobel Prize in 2023, was the first woman to win the accolade in her own right. Her work on the gender implications of the hours spent on paid work was neither fashionable nor a well-worn path for economists. It didn't deter her. Constitutional law expert Professor Megan Davis has spoken of her modest upbringing and being inspired by her mother's love of books and a copy of the Australian Constitution to pursue a stellar legal career – and help draft the Uluru Statement from the Heart.

Even if others have already taken the road, the sheer scarcity of female leaders means they get over-scrutinised, and know they have to work out a way of operating that calibrates around expectations (another reason why telling women to just 'be authentic' is dangerous). It took some time, and fine tuning, for director and former CEO Susan Lloyd-Hurwitz to decide what kind of leader she was, particularly as an introvert. Doing it in the way she did emerged over time and was partly in her personality. The image of a leader is highly entwined with the power and likability conundrum, she explained to me in an interview.

There's a really fine line that women have to tread between power and likability. And you can do both. But it's definitely a hard thing to do … and I was very much a servant leader, I set direction but for the rest of the time, I was just gently influencing … a servant leader is quite a different model than 'here's the heroic come to lead the troops' type.

I was really trying to mirror that the responsibility of a leader is not to accumulate wealth for themselves, or power. But to add to the whole system for everybody. I tried the same when I was the president of The Property Council, it was tricky too, because there were a lot of egos around the table. Trying to be a servant leader in that environment was challenging.

Lloyd-Hurwitz also decided to get input on her performance through 360-degree reviews (which use feedback from co-workers, reporting staff and customers), 'because even with all the best intentions you don't know what impact you're having on people necessarily and need someone to look at it'. While anyone in leadership can use these approaches, women in authority are also walking a tightrope between behavioural expectations that are rarely faced by men in authority.

Channel the anger

Instead of trying to curb emotions, women I spoke to often have used them as motivation to help challenge sexism and the masculine straitjacket. Occasionally this has been propelled by righteous fury, which has long been seen as a taboo for women. Yet it can lead to life-changing decisions. Using anger instead of suppressing it can get things done, with evidence that it can help motivate us to achieve goals despite the pressure for women to stay even-tempered.[1]

When Julia Gillard decided to deliver that speech, she was driven by a number of emotions and one of them was anger. But it was a cold anger, she pointed out to the audience at the tenth anniversary event in 2022. It drove her to list a devastating string of sexist comments by Opposition leader Tony Abbott that had been compiled by her staff. It didn't take them long, she remarked. It was a line-in-the-sand decision, and many thousands of women seemed to think so too.

Conforming to what has been acceptable would have meant some of the most famous examples of women's leadership and trailblazing might never have happened. It's also become clear that many key contributions from women who dutifully supported famous men have been ignored and only unearthed in recent years. Anna Funder's book *Wifedom* examined the life of Eileen Blair, the overlooked wife of author George Orwell. Interviewed about the book, Funder said women should be annoyed about inequality and not fobbed off with assurances that some have it better than others.[2]

Sheer exasperation as an incentive in making decisions came up, too. I quoted University of Technology Sydney legal academic and author Ramona Vijeyarasa at the beginning of the book about her work on women leading governments, and in developing a gender legislative index. She told me she shares my deep frustration about the lack of progress and that made her decide to focus on and spell out the impact of women running governments.

> If women aren't at those decision-making tables, we are not playing a part in shaping the way the world is and deciding how we want the world to look in the future. You know, the obvious examples being around climate decision-making but even finance, accountability, inequities across nations, we're not there in those spaces. That was what really motivated me to look at it. I was so surprised by how few people are mapping how few women have made it, and I suppose it's because of the way politics works. It changes so quickly.

Decisions about the focus of her work, which examined women leaders in South-East Asia, revealed practical insights on how women can support and encourage efforts to see change in politics and business. Women need spaces where they're supported to come together, and women can be good at that, she pointed out. In research on women in politics in Sri Lanka, and other countries, Vijeyarasa saw the way party politics can make it hard for more solidarity between older successful female politicians and the younger generation.

But she observed it is possible in Jakarta, where women in all parts of politics come together informally at a restaurant every few months just to talk about how to deal with common experiences, while sharing knowledge. 'It was a true experience of solidarity and Australia could learn from this', she added.

Decisions under pressure

There are few better Australian examples of sustained, effective decision-making I've seen than the work of activist Wendy McCarthy. She started her career as a teacher, ran women's reproductive organisation Family Planning, and has fought for women's rights for decades, through numerous campaigns, and during a long board career. Her influence has cut across the organisational to philanthropic and propelling social change on women's rights.

A skill in making fast decisions came from having her back against the wall a few times, she says. It's also been about strategic activism on crucial social issues like abortion. Watching what was happening in the US when abortion rights were overturned by the Supreme Court, she marshalled a group to campaign for the removal of abortion from the Criminal Code in NSW in 2019. This was driven by concern that something similar could happen in Australia without action, and that the way to campaign was to treat abortion as a key women's health concern. A core group strategised, made plans and arranged rallies: the well-executed strategy worked.

At an earlier point in her life she made a decision to join her first board, in the higher education sector, after initially balking at the prospect. Giving herself 24 hours to think about it, she realised that the minister inviting her was making a good point: 'He asked why was I standing outside hacking away at a system and having not a lot of impact, when I could be part of the system and change it?' she recalled when we spoke.

McCarthy's experience, plus her decision-making skills and the capacity to deal with the consequences, led her to join the ABC board a few years later. Sitting on big boards with big responsibilities provided marvellous experience for learning to prioritise and bring nuance to issues. 'You do have to learn the decision-making process and to trust your own instinct', she adds. When she went to the ABC, 'It was a very tumultuous time. We had three women on the board and we were there to represent women, and to think about women along with our individual responsibilities as a director'. That made a big difference to board discussions and decisions.

Former Australia Post CEO Christine Holgate is still often asked about her 2020 decision to staunchly defend herself to the prime minister and chair of Australia Post after criticism for giving some of her executives luxury watches as a bonus. Now CEO of transport company Team Global Express, she is clear about what was at stake when she appeared to answer questions at a 2021 Senate hearing.

Her mental health was fragile, and it was incredibly stressful to go to parliament to give evidence, she told me. There were armed guards to get her into the building and her public profile was being shredded, with cartoons depicting her as a prostitute. The gender abuse was relentless and blatant. But she also knew she couldn't live with herself if she hadn't taken a stand against the bullying. And support from female employees at Australia Post, as well as from around Australia, made her feel she had to take a stand.

> What I learned from that process was when that report
> came out, and when I gave evidence, even though
> people only got a snapshot into what happened, loads
> of people felt I had been wronged. And then they were

waiting for that [Senate Inquiry] report – it was almost their relief, as well as my relief.

Her decision has inspired and motivated many women around the country – and possibly alerted some men to the consequences of misusing their power.

Listening

One of the insights about decision-making that many women shared was about listening. For Holgate it's a key part of the job, and she loves talking to customers and employees, as well as mentors.

> I think they give you the best ideas. It doesn't mean that I'm not decisive because I'm actually a very decisive person. What it means is I actually form my views by talking, listening, consulting. And yet people think if you're a listener, if you do that, it's a sign of weakness.

A failure to listen to First Nations women has a long history, according to filmmaker and advocate Rachel Perkins, whose father, Charles Perkins, played a pivotal role in the civil rights movement in Australia, heading a series of famous 'Freedom Rides' through NSW in the mid-1960s, and becoming the first Indigenous leader of a government department. Rachel Perkins spoke at a 2023 forum arranged by Women for the Voice about their key role in the referendum campaign. Women have lots of experience of not being listened to, Perkins said. In their professional, and personal lives, it's been difficult to be heard and that motivated her decision to drive the campaign.

> I think we know that when you do listen, you make
> better decisions. So I think for women we can more
> easily empathise with the position of First Nations
> people who have been trying to be heard because
> they have the solutions in their communities, but
> government doesn't listen. So it's all about doing
> things better. Listening … I think can play a big
> role. We know that women are hugely influential in
> their families and in their homes. Gender equity is so
> important for the women from my community, and
> Alice Springs, who are much talked about, but not
> talked to.

Sam Mostyn (now Governor-General), who moderated the 2023 forum, reminded the audience that gender representation was carefully thought through by those taking part in the Uluru dialogues, which tells us something about how good decisions get made when women are at the table.

A couple of years before this event, when she was president of Chief Executive Women, Mostyn made a pivotal decision to address the National Press Club about the care economy (mentioned in Chapter 2). It was a call for serious attention to an arena that employs mainly women in low-paid but essential work. The 2021 landmark speech made a clear connection between the overlooked and undervalued care sector and economic success, and called for long overdue recognition of what women contribute to society. It reframed a debate that has often ignored the poor conditions in the highly feminised sector, and that females do most unpaid care, while urging women to make different 'choices' and retrain despite the barriers they would face.

Coming out of COVID lockdowns, there was a particular moment for attention to and disruption of the status of this critical sector, she recalled when we spoke in 2023.

> There was a moment to grab here and talk about it on the national agenda. And that's what the Press Club idea came from. It was to actually put it into context, and make it a substantial national, social and economic topic. And I worked for several months on the actual content of the speech to try to have a narrative that covered all of the various parts of the system, and to try and tell a story.

COVID had shown how much care matters, she recalled, and how heavily this country is leveraged to care, most of which is done by women.

> And that's why the speech goes through this and why there was a moment where we finally saw the economic and social value of women's work. We had this enormous explosion of women talking about how much more efficient they would be, and that work from home was actually something that would change the whole nature of who participated. It was telling a story about a society and what we can do and to imagine a world where we were sorting these things out – and this was a moment to grab.

The feedback from women around the country was profound: we feel like we're finally being seen, many told Mostyn. Not a lot of men commented – although NSW treasurer at the time, Matt Kean, got in touch and set up a Women's Economic Opportunities Review chaired by Mostyn, which ended up committing $10 billion to childcare and the preschool system. The impact didn't end there, with a focus on improving outcomes in the sector. Mostyn also chaired the 2023 Women's Economic Equality Taskforce for the federal government, which has made a series of recommendations on short- and longer-term policies from applying a gender lens to spending and the budget.

Deciding to tackle privilege

The CEO of Media Diversity Australia, Mariam Veiszadeh, arrived in Australia as a refugee from Afghanistan. An early interaction with an ESL (English as a second language) teacher, who pushed her out of her comfort zone, made her decide to give school debating a try. She nailed it, and eventually qualified as a lawyer, before turning her passion for racial and gender equity into a full-time job leading Media Diversity Australia.

She recalls researching a TEDx talk on privilege and being struck by the painfully slow rate of change in gender and cultural diversity in leadership. Her decision to take on the role at Media Diversity Australia was about a drive to trigger basic change in what we all see and hear on our screens. It's not only about appointing women or culturally diverse women into these decision-making roles, but having the scaffolding and the structural support to ensure they thrive.

When we spoke in 2023, she said women continue to face a potent mix of sexism, racism and pigeon-holing about class – even when they have authority.

> So you're kind of pushing up against a structure. You're riding a bike on a road that was not made for you. And the intersectional layer amplifies this disadvantage ... something I haven't talked about publicly is the racism I've faced fairly recently, when you're climbing into leadership roles. Not in this role, but in circles and in environments where they should know better and they should do better. And so there's just an assumption that if you get to a certain point and are pretty confident and you're getting up on stage, that you haven't faced those issues. But I do, and I think that that needs tackling and it's really hard to keep succeeding and thriving in that environment.

Taking that message to the people running many of Australia's major media outlets has been a part of her remit. Media Diversity has run a series of roundtables with this cohort to focus on recognising and addressing the everyday reality of racism. During a period of pressure around racism and bias in the media, including the 2023 resignation from the ABC of well-known Indigenous journalist Stan Grant, and the dismissal of journalist Antoinette Lattouf from her casual ABC radio presenter role, Veiszadeh has been using her experience to help change outcomes for intersectional employees and challenge the sector to do better.

Deciding with empathy

You cannot become a CEO or a senior executive without really well-honed decision-making skills, particularly when stressed, Miriam Silva, financial services executive and director explained to me. She's faced lots of critical moments in her career, including dealing with the SARS outbreak when she worked for ANZ in Hong Kong.

> Everyone's worst behaviour comes out under pressure, but when you've had a really good grounding in decision-making, that's where the best of you comes out. And I think as a woman, that's where the best of a woman can come out, under pressure, because you can bring a different style. It's not as aggressive and the energy is not so aggressive. And you can get to an outcome, and everybody comes with you.

During her time at the bank, she attended a leadership course, which had a major impact on how she approached her career decisions. It helped her understand that you're in control of the impact you and your decisions have on others, and how to use that to be better rather than to serve your own purpose.

Honing those decision-making skills has allowed her to build a board career for several organisations she cares deeply about – including InTouch Multicultural Centre Against Family Violence, Art Gallery of South Australia and Malek Fahd Islamic School (NSW). These roles have seen her at the decision-making table at the toughest of times – such as finding ways to help migrant women facing soaring levels of domestic violence during the peak of COVID lockdowns.

She's realistic and optimistic about the future of women's leadership because she thinks younger women are better equipped. 'I think the younger generation gives me hope. And we're also there to support them', she told me. That's also why having women from a range of racial backgrounds in leadership matters so much – it's far more than optics or ticking a box, but about having leaders who understand and champion the interests of the most vulnerable in the workplace who don't have the power to speak up.

In a recent role, Silva explained how a young female employee, who wears the hijab, walked into the office one day in distress. A man on the train had verbally abused her and she had been frozen in fear. 'And she walked into the office and burst into tears in my arms. When she calmed down, I said, "OK, let's talk about this". That's a young woman, wearing a hijab, who has that experience coming to work on a train in Sydney.' She just wanted to get to work safely, do her job and feel included, Silva said.

Making decisions hinges on consultation and inclusion for Sam Turner, a DEI (diversity, equity and inclusion) leader and currently chief people officer at law firm Allens. She often thinks about the lens that might be missing from a discussion, she explained when we spoke.

I think also, being LGBTQ+ does give you a different lens for decision-making. It has the potential to enable you to be more inclusive, because you have a lived experience of being 'other' … For me personally, I have a heightened level of empathy. The ability to think and observe what would it feel like if I was in your shoes. As opposed to compassion, which I see a lot of from the dominant majority. That's 'I feel sorry for you'. But I don't want you to feel sorry. I want you to think about how I feel, what it's like to live through my lens. Overall however, when you look at decision-making, anywhere, I think we're still not invited to the table as often.

That includes boards and executive leadership, which are still dominated by cis straight men, with similar education and background who therefore mostly think the same way, Turner says. Having worked across several large organisations in DEI, she has had some really good role models. She likes talking through an issue and finds board experience invaluable because you've got to build consensus, with often incredibly divergent views. It's also just about asking lots of questions. 'But I think, with decision-making there are just fewer role models. And we do look to women, we do look to people who are similar to us. We're hardwired to do that. And I also think our decisions are questioned more', she added.

The upside of being underestimated

Dr Lisa Chaffey made a supremely tactical decision when she started school and was the only kid in a wheelchair. She made friends with the coolest girl in the class. It was a deliberate step and paid off for Chaffey, now a Paralympian who sits on a number of boards. She says she found herself in leadership roles during her career by accident rather than by design. Although she trained as an occupational therapist and worked in mental health, she found it a little bit difficult to get her first job.

> Because I was in a wheelchair I was under-underestimated when I was in the helping profession. I should have been someone who needed help, not someone who was helping. So that was my first taste of 'Oh, hang on a minute. I need to actually project myself for people to see me'. So I think very early on in my career I decided to have an approach which was a little bit more assertive, but I felt comfortable with and look for very quick wins ... to have some successes that people can see whether they were successes that I valued or successes that would be about long-term effect. That was irrelevant.

When it came to her decision to run as an independent MP, Kylea Tink explained it was timing, and knowing she had the skills and trusted her judgement that tipped the scales. But what originally set her on the path to Parliament House was listening to a decision by former prime minister Scott Morrison to open a new coal power plant in NSW.

> It triggered a collision in my brain of not only my personal passion area, which was a sustainable, safe environment for my kids, but my business brain, and thinking, 'That's a bad decision'. And if I reflect on it, the other thing that was so important about that time in my life is that I trusted I had the experience to make that call. I finally felt like, 'No, I've worked

in business for 30 years now, I've run businesses, I've seen how things work. That is a bad business decision'.

The other deciding factor for Tink was her age: she had recently turned 50, and felt she knew what she was talking about in a way her younger self wouldn't have. During her career, the expectation had been, 'I needed to prove I could do a job before I owned it'. That didn't seem to be the same expectation for the men she worked with, who were encouraged to apply before they had the experience. But having more experience and trusting her skills helped make a significant decision that ended up with a seat in parliament.

Learning from decision-makers

Nareen Young has made plenty of decisions about policies and programs to address the lack of diversity in Australian workplaces – and learnt early on how to stand her ground. Now Professor for Indigenous Policy at the Jumbunna Institute for Indigenous Education and Research, and Associate Dean Indigenous Leadership and Engagement at University of Technology Sydney, she also spent many years running the Diversity Council of Australia. Growing up, and throughout her school years at St George Girls High School, it was just expected that you would make decisions, she explained to me. An early career decision to work for the union movement was pivotal as she watched women in the sector at the top of their game.

I was surrounded by amazing trade union women
as a young woman, was mentored and nurtured by
them, and I watched them and it was really hard, but
they did not back down. No, they just showed their
tenacity. That early activism in the labour movement,
that has paid off. You know, when I first went into
the Australian Services Union, for example, they had
a vice-president women position and that was in the
early 1990s, which of course wasn't just given, but was
a direct result of women's demands. I'm constantly
amazed to see women in other forums politely asking
for these things only now.

Of course, role models like these also show how women
bring a blend of personal and professional experience to
the table – and use those resources to help identify the key
issues that may otherwise be overlooked in workplaces,
communities and across society.

It's all in the timing

Sometimes, of course, decisions aren't about taking the
plunge but actually saying no. Laing O'Rourke's Director –
Legal, Risk & Delivery, Annabel Crookes, who I spoke to
about the gender balance on the Australian Construction
Industry Culture Taskforce (Chapter 6), told me she decided
not to become president of the association when she was
first asked.

I was nominated for the president position last year
[2022], and I had been asked to do it probably a year
before that but had said no, because at that stage I still
looked around that boardroom and thought, 'I don't
really feel like I could make change'. But once you
develop the relationships, and you see other people
that are like you, and you look across the room and
someone's nodding in agreement, men and women, it's
not just the females, there's a real sense of camaraderie.
You can have much more of a sense that you can
create change. So now I am the president and we have
another woman as one of our vice-presidents, Meg
Redwin, in the executive leadership team. We also
have diverse representation on the board – not just
men and women, but leaders with diverse backgrounds
including engineers, lawyers, HR professionals,
accountants, architects.

On the other hand, a big decision can emerge from realising
you're already taking on a role, and it's time to go further.
Mona Mohamed decided to found Community Support
Services (CSS) in Sydney's Bankstown in 2017 after realising
she'd already spent a lot of time advocating for women in
the community, mostly from migrant backgrounds, who
were struggling to negotiate basic services.

Many had never had a bank account or knew anything
about dealing with Centrelink. It was a turning point for
Mohamed, who was already a busy parent of six children,
and now it feels as though CSS found her and not the other
way around, she explained to me. She had the skills to
advocate for the many women in her neighbourhood who

felt isolated even in a big city and came from 30 different language groups.

> To an extent, these women believe that they can't make decisions, while financial abuse is quite common. Due to their language barriers, due to not knowing the law, due to fear that if they can't handle the finances, or their Centrelink card and the family tax benefit, they'll be sent back home.

In fact, despite being brainwashed that they are incapable, many of them are adept decision-makers, she adds. 'They make so many decisions around the home, around the children, around how to stretch the budget. And they are leaders in their own right too', she told me. CSS runs a foodbank, the Village Pantry, workshops and education courses, and school holiday programs. Seeing women learn key skills and support each other were the most uplifting aspects of what CSS does, and while Mohamed has over-come plenty of obstacles in setting it up, she has never looked back. Recognition of the impact she is having on women's capacity to make a living is on the increase, both in her local community and among funders.

Deciding to go against the grain

When she was first giving birth, Wendy McCarthy had to resist advice from medical staff to ban her husband, Gordon, from the delivery room. A few decades ago, it simply wasn't the done thing for men to be present, but she decided to put her foot down and Gordon was by her side when she had her daughter. Countless women have people like Wendy to thank for the change that started to happen when she and other women made that decision, and for ensuring a particularly epic and painful process became a bit more bearable with a lot more bonding.

Deciding to go against convention came up a few times in these conversations. That's what led Julie Chai to set up the Asian Leadership Project in 2017. Growing up, she explained, there was a glass ceiling at home: in her Chinese Cambodian family, leadership was reserved for men; women were expected to do the cooking and cleaning and get married. Her parents did not have Australian workplace culture experience, and the lessons instilled in her were about working hard and saving money, which didn't prepare her for leadership.

Deciding to launch the Project was based on market research, relevant experience and identifying a gap to fill. Not everyone was supportive of her decision – a trusted member of her network told her to slow down and think small.

> I was completely shocked, given this was my trusted colleague. I just said to myself, 'I can deliver this and I know the right people, the organisations that support me, I'm going to push forward. And I will not slow down and I'm not thinking small'. And then after I launched, the same colleague, sent me a LinkedIn message saying, 'I'm sorry for saying what I did. Because you've just proved me wrong'.

Chai's commitment proved to be a good call, and the organisation has grown consistently, increasing its membership and corporate partners.

When Caroline Ford set up a feminist book club for scientists in 2018, she was in uncharted territory. She said it was a quick decision that drew together her interest in books, plus the latest ideas in science and feminism. The STEMMinist Book Club now has members from around the world and features discussions with well-known authors such as Angela Saini.

> I'm so glad I did it, because I felt like that was the point in my career where I realised I didn't have to follow a stereotype of what I thought a scientist or a professor was – very serious and focused on their academic pursuits at all times. I felt that it was OK to embrace and celebrate the other side of me which was really interested in reading and feminism, equity and arts and comedy – and that all of that actually made me a better scientist. I think that that experience of the book club and meeting an incredible network of like-minded individuals really changed my thinking and as I've become more senior, and now I'm a professor, I've realised that.

Calling it out

A decision to speak about a lifetime of endometriosis pain and the impact of menopause to several hundred people at the Women in Mining conference in 2023 was not taken lightly, Libby Lyons, former director of WGEA, told me. It was partly because her whole life, she'd had to remain silent – just like most women – about the health issues that have impeded her daily life. Women were always carrying a hell of a lot more than men, and so she thought 'We've got to talk openly about this'.

> Women have to soldier on … I just think we've got to get it out there and talk more about the difference in physical and health issues that women experience compared to men. Because if we don't talk about it, we're never going to change the status quo and women will continue to have to 'soldier on' at work in pain and discomfort. It is the first time I've every spoken about it. We have to start to acknowledge that there are physical differences the we have to take into account, and those examples show that actually we're not the weakest sex.

Confronting the reality of sexism remains a courageous and at times risky decision for women, no matter their seniority. I was struck by how Amanda Blanc, CEO of UK insurer Aviva, talked about her stand on poor behaviour. She publicly cancelled Aviva's membership of the Confederation of British Industry (CBI) in mid-2023 after allegations of sexual harassment at the body.

Blanc is also on the board of BP, which sacked CEO Bernard Looney for 'serious misconduct' and personal relationships with colleagues. Speaking up comes with a price: Blanc has been criticised for her actions and accused of playing gender politics, and a couple of years ago she faced sexist abuse by shareholders at Aviva's AGM. That hasn't stopped her. Blanc has said that she wants to be known for what she achieves as a business leader but had realised, 'You have a responsibility. With senior positions comes a responsibility to be able to call out'.[3]

Next generation of decision-makers

Lawyer and Wiradjuri woman Kishaya Delaney didn't make a decision to become a leader, but a tragedy in her family did motivate her to use her influence while she was still at school. Losing her younger brother in a car accident, she became an advocate for organ and blood donation. But being called a leader didn't sit easily with her.

> From quite a young age I was into advocacy. I think
> because of that, people are telling you that you're a
> leader but I felt a disconnect. I think what I saw as a
> leader and what I was, it's hard to join the dots there.
> I was much more [focused on] what you are doing,
> rather than what people say you are doing. I didn't
> feel influential.

After leaving school she went to university in Newcastle, then did a series of internships with Westpac/BT, before joining Herbert Smith Freehills and becoming a solicitor with a keen focus on First Nations issues and the lack of Indigenous perspectives. Her approach to making decisions comes from working in teams and through the examples of mentors, she adds. Her team is all women in the pro bono area; it's a very flat structure, with collective decision-making and valuing of opinions. Younger people these days feel more empowered and their perspective is more valued, she said, and many feel 'who will speak on my behalf if not us?'

Seeing how a younger generation navigate an increasingly complex web of intersectional dynamics fills LaTrobe University academic Maria Pallotta-Chiarolli with hope. She teaches and works with many groups to analyse and challenge systems and power structures she told me. 'A younger generation has grown up in a much more diverse environment, they are learning differently and they're much more aware of intersectionalities,' she said.

> So these women are tapping into information. They've got their own sites and then they learn hopefully, how this all works, so they don't want to be part of these systems. They're hoping to change it or shift it and reconstruct something. I'm seeing that a lot. Even wonderful Ash Barty – their idea of success is not built on how many tennis trophies and how many millions of accolades … And that's a huge shift from that keep climbing, keep climbing and give up everything else at all costs.

Onward and upward

Women might not always be credited with decision-making gravitas, but a lot of them sure have it. They know how to call the shots while steering personal, professional and even national agendas. Many of these remarkable women haven't pursued a well-worn path but forged their own way because they've had to, particularly if they are from further marginalised groups.

Over-emotional? Afraid of risk? Indecisive? Inefficient? It's not how I'd describe the way these women make a call – quite the opposite in fact. It's time we heard more about these stories to really break the boss bias. Their responses didn't suggest a winning formula, but showed how complex it is to factor in gender bias, scrutiny and double standards. They often had to assess how their decisions would be seen in a way most men wouldn't think twice about. Yet as they explained, they had no trouble setting their path, despite being underestimated, and were very aware but unfazed by stereotypes or pressure to conform and stay in their lane. They just went ahead anyway.

The end of delusions

The marginalising of women from critical decision-making is neither inevitable nor intractable. But as the seven steps in this book reveal, any realistic hope of changing outcomes must start with breaking through the real and uncomfortable problem of rigid gender stereotypes and bias. The evidence set out here clearly shows attempts to close the leadership gender gap until now have made very little difference. Delusions of progress have protected the power status quo, and held women back. It's time to focus on addressing the cause, not the symptoms, of the disadvantage keeping half the world's population out of power.

Once you start seeing the real picture, you can't stop noticing it. As I finished writing this book in late 2023, the 28 participants for the Conference of Parties Climate Change Summit, COP29, hosted by Azerbaijan, were announced: 28 men. This is despite women being acknowledged as most at risk from climate change, and increasingly holding relevant leadership roles from NGOs to research bodies and in government.

Just a couple of months before reading about COP29, I heard Australian business leader Michael Chaney tell an audience of 1200 at the Women in Mining WA conference that in ten to 20 years, 50 per cent of CEOs would be women. While I admire the optimism, women currently hold less than a quarter of those roles across the economy and just 9 per cent of ASX300 CEO jobs.

The rhetoric and reality gap can't be bridged with platitudes about the problem simply resolving itself or telling women to get their act together. Sexism is a slippery beast that never disappeared but has changed over time. In recent years, women have been told to provide the 'business case' for gender equity, to lean in, speak up and to hang on to our jobs with gritty ambition while doing the housework and caring. Many of us came to the party on all fronts – and yet the outlook at the top barely changed.

That's what my analysis reveals: it's time for a new story about gender equity that doesn't dodge but engages with the cause of the problem. It means focusing on reality and data, not the 'she'll be right' gender-washing narrative; facing up to how bias and backlash operate instead of fobbing it off or minimising it; replacing traditional and stifling ideas about who makes effectives leaders with new models; taking seriously and preventing micro-aggressions; removing bias in systems; and elevating women's skill as decision-makers.

It's a lot, but I'm hopeful. When women are in power, the agenda shifts. It was dedicated and diverse women who got national paid parental leave over the line, the Respect@Work legislation enacted, and the publication of employers' gender pay gaps, who spoke out about bullying, sexual harassment, domestic violence and consent. While progress across the economy has been disjointed, some of the workplaces I've profiled show the opposite is true. It's a reminder that the needle can be moved quickly if there's commitment and women at the top.

These remarkable women have also made me think

again about finally upending the definition of a great boss. When I discussed this with trans woman Sally Goldner, she said both former New Zealand prime minister Jacinda Ardern and Julia Gillard were strong leaders who brought qualities associated with men and women to their roles.

> This is where trans and gender diverse people, when we're valued, what we do with diversity can add so much value … we do transcend the gender binary, and that's all of trans women, trans men and beyond the binary people. And we can see through these artificial barriers of gender, and just try to go beyond them and just be better people, and therefore better leaders.

Dismantling intersectional barriers for women is key to finding new leadership models – and for younger women particularly, it's a no brainer. They expect a different way of operating and leading, not a female replica of the current privileged, white, male power group.

That's the point of breaking bias – to create different ways to lead. As US feminist Gloria Steinem famously explained, feminism isn't about getting a bigger slice of the pie but baking a new pie. The recipe is starting to emerge as old leadership stories and formulae are rewritten. The saying that history is written by the victors, attributed to Winston Churchill, has motivated many women who have been increasingly writing their own histories, and new versions of neuroscience, the arts, anthropology and archaeology. They remind us women have always been making decisions, and driving social change, but their efforts were sidelined or rendered invisible.

Coming up with an alternative is possible because the latest research reminds us that patriarchy is a construct, not a natural division of power. Matrilineal societies still exist. UK author of *The Patriarchs*, Angela Saini, found women around the world have always fought male domination – and sometimes have had much more input in running societies. The idea that biological difference explains a massively exploitative power system distracts us from how precarious it actually is, she writes[1].

> When the grip of male power seems intractable, it
> may well feel as though it has been this way forever.
> Political leaders routinely invoke 'tradition' and'
> nature' when clamping down on women's rights: this
> is how it's always been, they claim, so this is how it
> should stay. But history tells a different story … The
> norms that a society follows are constructed, they are
> built. Women's rights and freedoms weren't missing
> in deep time. Just like in the present, they had to have
> been destroyed.[2]

Bias has been blinding us to the real story about who can and should be running the world. Women have never been so desperately needed at the table in every forum. As author Anna Funder explained, 'There is not one place on the planet where women as a group have the same power, freedom, leisure or money as their male partners'.[3] A wealthy and well-educated place like Australia should do much better – and occasionally there's a glimpse of what's possible.

I never thought a women's football team could galvanise the good fight for equity. In a country where sport is a cultural touchstone and regularly dominates the national conversation, the impact of the Matildas football team, along with women's professional teams in rugby, cricket and AFL, on smashing stereotypes is hard to overestimate.

It's an arena where you can show what equality looks like in the hardest, most immovable of Australian idioms, the first woman AFL commissioner (now Governor-General), Sam Mostyn, told me. We need to keep looking at all the factors that lead to inequality, set out our ambitions and not stop.

Most women I spoke to said the same thing, no matter their jobs, age or background. They have no intention of giving up the fight for women's rights and accountability for slow progress into decision-making jobs. They know that this has never been a straightforward movement, and that in some ways, women worldwide are just beginning the hardest part of the struggle for power. But just like the Matildas, we will keep going #tilitsdone.

Notes

Unless noted otherwise, all interviews were conducted by the author in 2023.

Introduction

1   World Economic Forum, Global Gender Gap Report 2023, 20 June 2023 <www.weforum.org/reports/global-gender-gap-report-2023/digest>.
2   Tonkov, P, 'Gender gap in home cooking grows', *Gallup*, 30 October 2023 <news.gallup.com/opinion/gallup/512918/gender-gap-home-cooking-grows.aspx>.
3   Deloitte, 'Breaking the norm: Unleashing Australia's economic potential', *Deloitte*, 14 November 2022 <www.deloitte.com/au/en/services/economics/perspectives/breaking-norm-unleashing-australia-economic-potential.html>.
4   Unless noted otherwise, all quotes are from interviews conducted by the author in 2023.

Chapter 1 – Replacing over-optimism with reality and action

1   Plan International, 'Gender Compass report', 13 September 2023 <www.plan.org.au/our-work/gender-compass/>.
2   Brancatisano, E, 'In a big year for women, here's where Australians really stand on gender equality', *SBS News*, 13 September 2023 <www.sbs.com.au/news/article/where-australia-stands-on-gender-equality/yn4goo7bj>.
3   Chief Executive Women, 'CEW Senior Executive Census 2023', 26 September 2023 <cew.org.au/advocacy-and-research/cew-2023-senior-executive-census/>.
4   Diehl, A, Dzubinski, L, & Stephenson, A, 'New research reveals the 30 critiques holding women back that men will never hear', *Fast Company*, 2 May 2023 <www.fastcompany.com/90889985/new-research-reveals-critiques-holding-women-back-from-leadership-that-most-men-will-never-hear>.
5   World Economic Forum, 'Global gender gap report 2023: Key findings', 20 June 2023 <www.weforum.org/reports/global-gender-gap-report-2023>.
6   Priestley, A, 'It will take 131 years to close the global gender gap and progress is stalling', *Women's Agenda*, 22 June 2023 <womensagenda.com.au/latest/it-will-take-131-years-to-close-the-global-gender-gap-and-progress-is-stalling/>.
7   UN Human Development Reports, '2023 Gender Social Norms Index', 12 June 2023 <hdr.undp.org/content/2023-gender-social-norms-index-gsni#/indicies/GSNI>.
8   World Bank, 'New data show massive, wider than expected global gender gap', World Bank Press Release, 4 March 2024 <www.worldbank.org/en/news/press-release/2024/03/04/new-data-show-massive-wider-than-expected-global-gender-gap>.

9   Yerushalmy, J, 'After Ardern, Marin and Sturgeon is female representation in politics going backwards?' *The Guardian*, 2 April 2023 <www.theguardian.com/world/2023/apr/06/after-ardern-marin-and-sturgeon-is-female-representation-in-politics-going-backwards>.

10   Shalal, A, 'Women leaders sidelined at multinational organisations, new study shows', Reuters, 7 March 2023 <www.reuters.com/business/women-leaders-sidelined-multilateral-organizations-new-study-shows-2023-03-06/>.

11   Boecker, B, 'It's a lonely place: Iceland PM Karin Jakobsdottir on the decline in female world leaders', Women's Agenda, 25 September 2023 <womensagenda.com.au/politics/world/its-a-lonely-place-iceland-pm-katrin-jakobsdottir-on-the-decline-in-female-world-leaders/>.

12   Department of Prime Minister and Cabinet, 'National strategy to achieve gender equality: Discussion paper', 7 March 2023 <www.pmc.gov.au/resources/national-strategy-achieve-gender-equality-discussion-paper/current-state/leadership>.

13   Massola, J, 'Female secretaries, male chiefs of staff: Canberra's top political jobs dominated by men' *Sydney Morning Herald*, 30 May 2021 <www.smh.com.au/politics/federal/female-secretaries-male-chiefs-of-staff-canberra-s-top-political-jobs-dominated-by-men-20210528-p57w41.html>.

14   Workplace Gender Equality Agency, 'Australia's gender equality scorecard 2022–23', 8 November 2023 <www.wgea.gov.au/publications/australias-gender-equality-scorecard>.

15   Tamer, R, 'These are the Australian occupations that continue to be segregated by gender', *SBS News*, 31 January 2023 <www.sbs.com.au/news/article/these-are-the-australian-occupations-that-continue-to-be-segregated-by-gender/5f6vdu1j4>.

16   WGEA, 'Australia's gender scorecard 2022–23'.

17   Watermark Search International & Governance Institute Australia, '2023 Board Diversity Index', 3 April 2023 <www.watermarksearch.com.au/thought-leadership/2023-board-diversity-index>.

18   Heidrick & Struggles, 'Boards monitor US 2023', 7 March 2023 <www.heidrick.com/-/media/heidrickcom/publications-and-reports/board-monitor-us-2023.pdf>.

19   Department of Prime Minister and Cabinet, 'National strategy to achieve gender equality' n.d. <www.pmc.gov.au/resources/national-strategy-achieve-gender-equality-discussion-paper/current-state/leadership>.

20   Priestley, A, 'Men dominate public health leadership. A new network plans to change that', *Women's Agenda*, 26 June 2023 <womensagenda.com.au/life/health/men-dominate-public-health-leadership-a-new-network-plans-to-change-that/>.

21   Diversity Council of Australia, 'Culturally and racially marginalised women in leadership', 6 September 2023 <www.dca.org.au/research/culturally-and-racially-marginalised-carm-women-in-leadership>.

22   AAP & Multicultural Communities Council of NSW, the National Sikh Council of Australia (NSCA) and the Chinese Community Council of Australia, 'Premier's misogynist government exposed again', *Media Release*, 21 January 2023.

23   NSW Council of Social Service, 'Long way to the top', 1 March 2022
      <www.ncoss.org.au/wp-content/uploads/2022/03/NCOSS_
      LongWayToTheTop_FINAL.pdf>

24   O'Bannon, I, 'Progress of women in leadership is stalling', *CPA Practice
      Advisor*, 4 April 2023 <www.cpapracticeadvisor.com/2023/04/04/progress-
      of-women-in-leadership-is-stalling/78437/>

25   O'Bannon, 2023.

26   Walters, R. 'Gender washing: Seven kinds of marketing hypocrisy about
      empowering women', *The Conversation*, 18 June 2021 <theconversation.com/
      gender-washing-seven-kinds-of-marketing-hypocrisy-about-empowering-
      women-162777>.

27   Walter, R, 2021.

28   Fox, C, 'Reporting on International Women's Day', Women in Media
      Newsletter, 27 March 2023.

29   Lawson, F & Fensome, A, 'The gender pay gap app' <genderpaygap.app>.

30   Durkin, P, 'Australia's 50 highest paid CEOs', *Australian Financial
      Review*, 1 December 2023 <www.afr.com/work-and-careers/workplace/
      revealed-australia-s-50-highest-paid -ceos-in-2023-20231124-
      p5emmw#:~:text=Macquarie%20Group%20chief%20executive%20
      Shemara,third%20year%20in%20a%20row>.

31   Begeny, C & Ryan, M, 'Gender discrimination in the veterinary profession',
      University of Exeter and British Veterinary Association, November 2018
      <ore.exeter.ac.uk/repository/bitstream/handle/10871/36424/BVA%20
      Employers%20Study_Brief%20Report_Final%20Draft.pdf?sequence=1>.

32   Handsley-Davis, M, 'Doctor Who?', *Cosmos*, 22 March 2022.

33   Begeny & Ryan, 2018, p. 7.

34   Cox, J, 'Why it's getting harder for some women to report harassment',
      BBC Worklife, 4 June 2023 <www.bbc.com/worklife/article/20230615-why-
      its-getting-harder-for-some-women-to-report-harassment>.

35   Cox, 2023.

36   Chamorro-Premuzic, T, 'The business case for women in leadership', *Forbes*,
      2 March 2022 <www.forbes.com/sites/tomaspremuzic/2022/03/02/the-
      business-case-for-women-in-leadership/?sh=1d54a3339cbb>.

37   Vijeyarasa, R, '3 reasons why women leaders actually matter for women',
      The Conversation, 27 July 2022, <theconversation.com/3-reasons-why-
      women-leaders-actually-matter-for-women-183440>.

Chapter 2 – Breaking down the bias barriers

1   Jackson, A, 'Impact Economics and Policy Submission: The Senate Standing
      Committee on Community Affairs - Legislation Committee – Inquiry into
      the Paid Parental Leave Amendment (More support for working families)
      Bill 2023', 12 December 2023.

2   Workplace Gender Equality Agency, 'WGEA Gender Euqality Scorecard
      2022–23', 28 November 2023.

3   McNamara, S, 'How caring for kids grows skills that are directly transferable
      to paid work', *Women's Agenda*, 16 June 2023 <womensagenda.com.au/latest/
      how-caring-for-children-grows-skills-that-are-directly-transferable-to-paid-
      work/>.

4   Hsu, A, 'Women are earning more money. But they are still picking up a heavier load at home', NPR, 23 April 2023 <www.npr. org/2023/04/13/1168961388/pew-earnings-gender-wage-gap-housework-chores-child-care>.

5   Dinh, H, Welsh, J, & Strazdins, L, 'Work hour limits need to change for better mental health and gender equality', *The Conversation*, 2 February 2017 <theconversation.com/work-hour-limits-need-to-change-for-better-mental-health-and-gender-equality-71999>.

6   Kelly, S, 'If employers stop people working from home, one group will pay dearly', *Sydney Morning Herald*, 18 December 2023 <www.smh.com.au/national/if-employers-stop-people-working-from-home-one-group-will-pay-dearly-20231217-p5eryp.html>.

7   Tuohy, W, 'Fathers who share childcare face work and career setbacks', *Sydney Morning Herald*, 19 March 2023 <www.smh.com.au/national/fathers-who-share-childcare-face-work-discrimination-and-career-setbacks-20230316-p5csln.html>.

8   Meekes, J & Ruppaner, L, 'Flexible work arrangements help women but only if they are also offered to men', *The Conversation*, 8 March 2021 <theconversation.com/flexible-work-arrangements-help-women-but-only-if-they-are-also-offered-to-men-155882>

9   Ammerman & Groysberg, 2021, p. 21.

10   Ammerman & Groysberg, 2021, p. 48.

11   Lui, J, 'Women are held back at work due to 30 biases out of their control new study says', *CNBC*, 3 June 2023 <www.cnbc.com/2023/06/07/women-criticized-at-work-on-30-characteristics-says-study-of-female-leaders-.html>.

12   Green Carmichael, S, 'Goldin's Nobel Prize shows flexible work is key for women, despite what CEOs say', *Sydney Morning Herald*, 14 October 2023 <www.smh.com.au/business/workplace/goldin-s-nobel-prize-shows-flexible-work-is-key-for-women-despite-what-ceos-say-20231010-p5eazg.html>.

13   Sidic, S 'Toxic workplaces are the main reason women leave academic jobs', *Nature*, 20 October 2023 <www.nature.com/articles/d41586-023-03251-8>.

14   Gibson,C, 'Workplace discrimination is rife for pregnant women and working parents', *News from the University of South Australia*, August 2023 <www.unisa.edu.au/unisanews/2023/august/story2/>.

15   WGEA, 'New data shows Australian workers face a part-time promotion cliff', 15 November 2023 <www.wgea.gov.au/newsroom/New-data-Australian-workers-part-time-promotion-cliff>.

16   Cox, J, 'The trust crisis facing women leaders', *BBC Worklife*, 1 December 2022 <www.bbc.com/worklife/article/20221129-the-trust-crisis-facing-women-leaders>.

17   Price, J, 'What Berejiklian and Maguire tells us about the state of modern love', *Sydney Morning Herald*, 2 July 2023 <www.smh.com.au/lifestyle/life-and-relationships/what-berejiklian-and-maguire-tell-us-about-the-state-of-modern-love-20230703-p5dlgd.html>.

18   Corbyn, Z, 'Hungry judges dispense rough justice', *Nature*, 11 April 2011 <www.nature.com/articles/news.2011.227>.

19   Jesuit Social Services, 'Modelling respect and equality evaluation finds pilot program promotes change', 25 January 2024 <jss.org.au/news-and-media/our-

thinking/modelling-respect-and-equality-evaluation-finds-pilot-program-promotes-change/>.

20   Byrne, D, 'Social sponges: Gendered brain development comes from society, not biology', *Nature*, 13 March 2023 <www.nature.com/articles/d41586-023-00738-2>.

21   University of Southern California, 'When stressed, men charge ahead, women more careful, study finds', *ScienceDaily*, 4 June 2011 <www.sciencedaily.com/releases/2011/06/110603125103.htm>.

22   Wiersema, M & Mors, M, 'Research: How women improve decision making on boards', *HBR*, 17 November 2023 <hbr.org/2023/11/research-how-women-improve-decision-making-on-boards?tpcc=orgsocial_edit&utm_campaign=hbr&utm_medium=social&utm_source=linkedin>.

23   Lin,C & Gurcu, D, 'Women are risk takers, too: Busting gender myths in the startup space', *Insead Knowledge*, 6 March 2019 <knowledge.insead.edu/entrepreneurship/women-are-risk-takers-too-busting-gender-myths-start-space>.

24   Scale Investors website <scaleinvestors.com.au/>.

25   Workplace Gender Equality Agency, 'Higher education enrolments and graduate labour market statistics', 28 April 2021 <www.wgea.gov.au/resources/publications/higher-education-enrolments-and-graduate-labour-market-statistics>.

26   Vanguard, 'The rise of the female investor', September 2021 <www.vanguard.com.au/personal/learn/smart-investing/investing-strategy/rise-of-the-female-investor>.

27   Fox, C, 'Why women are the next big thing in personal finance', *The Australian*, 17 June 2021 <www.theaustralian.com.au%2Fbusiness%2Fthe-deal-magazine%2Fwhy-women-are-the-next-big-thing-in-personal-finance%2Fnews-story%d>.

28   Diehl, A, Dzubinski. L, & Stephenson, A, 'Women in leadership face ageism at every age', *HBR*, 16 June 2023 <hbr.org/2023/06/women-in-leadership-face-ageism-at-every-age>.

29   Sieghart, MA, *The Authority Gap*, Penguin Random House, 2021, p. 61.

30   Sieghart, 2021, p. 52.

31   Casselman, B, 'For women in economics, the hostility is out in the open', *New York Times*, 23 February 2021 <www.nytimes.com/2021/02/23/business/economy/economics-women-gender-bias.html>.

32   Danziger, P, 'As retail CEO turnover increases, women lose ground', *Forbes*, 6 January, 2024 <http://www.forbes.com/sites/pamdanziger/2024/01/06/as-retail-ceo-turnover-increases-women-lose-ground/?sh=70c174a4625d>.

33   Oakes, K, 'The invisible danger of the glass cliff', *BBC Future*, 7 February 2022 <www.bbc.com/future/article/20220204-the-danger-of-the-glass-cliff-for-women-and-people-of-colour>.

34   Hatch, P, 'James Hardie's CEO sacking highlights falling tolerance for workplace bullies', *Australian Financial Review*, 9 January 2022 <www.smh.com.au/business/companies/james-hardie-s-ceo-sacking-highlights-falling-tolerance-for-workplace-bullies-20220109-p59mvu.html>.

Chapter 3 – Tackling the elephant in the room: Backlash

1   Clarke, S & Aslandis, J, 'Young men now hold some of the most regressive attitudes towards gender. We can help change this', *Women's Agenda*, 14 June 2022 <womensagenda.com.au/latest/young-men-now-hold-some-of-the-most-regressive-attitudes-towards-gender-we-can-help-change-this>.

2   Chowdhury, I, 'Australia's young people are moving to the left, though young women are more progressive than men, reflecting a global trend', *The Conversation*, 5 February 2024.

3   Plan International, 'Gender Compass', *Plan International Australia*, 14 September 2023 <www.plan.org.au/wp-content/uploads/2023/09/GenderCompass_Report.pdf>.

4   Global Institute for Women's Leadership, 'International Women's Day 2022', March 2022 <www.kcl.ac.uk/giwl/assets/iwd-survey-2022.pdf>.

5   UN, '2023 Gender Social Norms Index', *UN Human Development Reports*, 12 June 2023 <hdr.undp.org/content/2023-gender-social-norms-index-gsni#/indicies/GSNI>.

6   FINSIA, 'The gender divide in financial services', October 2021 <www.womenonboards.net/womenonboards-AU/media/AU-PDFs/FINSIA-Gender-Divide-Financial-Serv-2021-Amended-embargo-until-11-59PM-AEDT-12Oct21-(1).pdf>.

7   Fox, C, 'It's no longer a gender pay gap, it's a yawning chasm', *The Big Smoke*, 19 October 2021 <thebigsmoke.com.au/2021/10/19/its-no-longer-a-gender-pay-gap-its-a-yawning-chasm>.

8   Workforce Gender Equality Agency, 'Employer gender pay gaps published first time', 27 February 2024.

9   FINSIA, 2021.

10   Kelly Services, 'The 2023 Kelly Workforce Report', 4 May 2023 <docs.kellyservices.com/story/rework-report-2023-gated/page/1?utm_source=au-press-release&utm_medium=referral&utm_campaign=2023-04_global_b2b_rework-report&utm_content=campaign_organic_pr_may-4-2023_australia>.

11   Haththotuwa, S, 'Major firms ditch diversity officers: Is this the end for corporate DEI?', *HR Grapevine*, 5 July 2023 <www.hrgrapevine.com/content/article/2023-07-04-production-studios-ditch-diversity-officers-are-they-non-essential>.

12   AHRI, 'The state of diversity, equity and inclusion in Australian workplaces 2023', 23 February 2023 <www.ahri.com.au/wp-content/uploads/DEI-Report-2023.pdf>.

13   Menasce Horowitz, J & Igielnik, R, 'A century after women gained the right to vote, majority of Americans see work to do on gender equality', Pew Research Centre, 7 July 2020 <www.pewresearch.org/social-trends/2020/07/07/a-century-after-women-gained-the-right-to-vote-majority-of-americans-see-work-to-do-on-gender-equality/>.

14   Flood, M, 'Challenging everyday sexism', *xyonline*, 12 June 2019 <xyonline.net/content/challenging-everyday-sexism>.

15   Fox, C, 'How can workplaces stop the scourge of sexual harassment?', *Company Director*, 1 June 2021 <www.aicd.com.au/organisational-culture/business-ethics/issues/how-can-workplaces-stop-the-scourge-of-sexual-harassment.html>.

16   Goldgrab, S, 'Use what we've learned from the pandemic to be a
      better male ally', *Forbes*, 22 February 2022 <www.forbes.com/sites/
      forbescoachescouncil/2022/02/22/use-what-weve-learned-from-the-
      pandemic-to-be-a-better-male-ally/?sh=402856a73130>

17   Goldgrab, 2022.

18   Tu, J, '"When men believe they are allies, women often disagree', *Women's
      Agenda*, 14 June 2023 <womensagenda.com.au/business/employers/when-
      men-believe-they-are-allies-women-often-disagree/>

19   Ferguson, K & Fox, C, *Women Kind*, Murdoch Books, Sydney 2018.

20   ANZSOG, 'How do we make public sector gender targets work?', *ANZSOG
      The Bridge*, 15 February 2023 <htertps://anzsog.edu.au/research-insights-and-
      resources/research/how-do-we-make-public-sector-gender-targets-work/>.

21   Khadem, N, 'Julia Szlakowski sparked AMP's "me too" moment, but it wasn't
      the first time she'd been forced out of a job due to sexual harassment', *ABC
      Online*, 23 July 2021 <http://www.abc.net.au/news/2021-07-21/sexual-
      harassment-amp-metoo-julia-szlakowski-amp-diversity/100307672>.

22   Le Beau, C, 'All along the pipeline men promote men', *UCLA Anderson
      Review*, 20 February 2020 <www.universityofcalifornia.edu/news/all-along-
      pipeline-men-promote-men>.

23   The 100% Project, '"Women in Finance: Beyond the numbers (2023)',
      August 2023 <the100percentproject.com.au/research/>.

24   WGEA, 'More women at the top proves better for business', 19 June 2020
      <www.wgea.gov.au/newsroom/more-women-at-the-top-proves-better-for-
      business>.

Chapter 4 – Learning new leadership lessons

1   Ferguson, K, *Head & Heart: The art of modern leadership*, Viking, 2023.

2   Caulkin, S, 'Will women leaders change the future of management?',
      Financial Times, 21 April 2022 <www.ft.com/content/6bf98d62-0ff4-4f19-
      a37d-e53f40abf6f2>.

3   Ammerman, C & Groysberg, B, *Glass Half Broken: Shattering the Barriers
      that Still Hold Women Back*, Harvard Business Review Press, 2021, p. 247.

4   Ammerman & Groysberg, 2021, p. 246.

5   Victoria University, 'Women find advancement through MBA', *Victoria
      University Online*, 15 July 2022 <online.vu.edu.au/blog/women-and-
      mba-programs#:~:text=While%20there's%20been%20significant%20
      progress,planned%20to%20earn%20an%20MBA>.

6   Ammerman & Groysberg, 2021, p. 246.

7   Ammerman & Groysberg, 2021, p. 247.

8   Ammerman & Groysberg, 2021, p. 240.

9   Ammerman & Groysberg, 2021, p. 28.

10   Ammerman & Groysberg, 2021, p. 241.

11   Smith, C, 'Diversity awareness in management education: survey results
      1995 research project', Edith Cowan University, 1995 <ro.ecu.edu.au/
      ecuworks/6880>.

12   Smith, C, 1995, p. 3.

13   Fitzsimmons, T & Callan, V, 'The diversity gap in leadership: what are
      we missing in current theorizing?', *The Leadership Quarterly*, vol. 31, no. 4,

August 2020, 101347 <www.sciencedirect.com/science/article/pii/
S1048984318307513>.

14 Fisher, AN, Ryan, MK, Schmader, T, & White, SL, Authenticity as an
Organisational Responsibility. Manuscript in preparation.

15 Orgad, S & Gill, R, *Confidence Culture*, Duke University Press, 2022, p. 74.

16 Orgad & Gill, 2022, p. 75.

Chapter 5 – Addressing everyday sexism

1   Castillo, L, 'Must-know self help industry statistics', *Gitnux*, 16 December
2023 <gitnux.org/self-help-industry-statistics/>.

2   Ammerman, C & Groysberg, B, *Glass Half Broken: Shattering the Barriers
that Still Hold Women Back*, Harvard Business Review Press, 2021, p. 185.

3   Gill, R & Orgad, S, 'The cult of confidence and why it doesn't help women',
Psyche, 24 May 2023 <psyche.co/ideas/the-cult-of-being-confident-and-
why-it-doesnt-help-women>.

4   Netchaeva, E, Kouchaki, M, & Sheppard, L, 'A man's (precarious) place:
Men's experienced threat and self-assertive reactions to female superiors',
Personality and Social Psychology Bulletin, vol. 41, no. 9, 2015, pp. 1247–1259
<doi.org/10.1177/0146167215593491>.

5   Risse, L, 'That advice to women to 'lean in', be more confident … it doesn't
help and data show it', *The Conversation*, 14 October 2020 <theconversation.
com/that-advice-to-women-to-lean-in-be-more-confident-it-doesnt-help-
and-data-show-it-146998>.

6   Chamorro-Premuzic, T, 'Why do so many mediocre men become leaders?'
Harvard Business Review, 22 August 2013 <hbr.org/2013/08/why-do-so-
many-incompetent-men>.

7   University College London, 'Men's overconfidence helps them reach top
jobs', *UCL News*, 24 April 2023 <cls.ucl.ac.uk/mens-overconfidence-helps-
them-reach-top-jobs/>.

8   Centre for Longitudinal Studies, 'Men's overconfidence helps them reach top
jobs', 24 April 2023 <https://cls.ucl.ac.uk/mens-overconfidence-helps-them-
reach-top-job>.

9   Saujani, R, "How can you overcome imposter syndrome? You don't', *Glamour*,
24 May 2023 <www.glamour.com/story/impostor-syndrome-isnt-a-
syndrome-its-a-scheme>.

10 Saujani, R, 'Imposter syndrome is a scheme: Reshma Saujani's
Smith College commencement address', 2023 <www.youtube.com/
watch?v=BoHDDgeQtlc>.

11 Women in Media, 'Women are severely under-represented in Australian
media', 15 February 2023 <www.womeninmedia.com.au/post/women-are-
severely-under-represented-in-australian-media>.

12 Adewunmi, B, 'Male TV presenter wears same suit for a year, does anyone
notice?', *The Guardian*, 18 November 2014 <www.theguardian.com/
lifeandstyle/womens-blog/2014/nov/17/male-tv-presenter-same-suit-year-
female-colleagues-judged>.

13 Shine, K, 'Interviews with journalists can seem daunting – but
research shows 80% of respondents report a positive experience',
The Conversation, 2 March 2023 <theconversation.com/interviews-with-

journalists-can-seem-daunting-but-new-research-shows-80-of-subjects-report-a-positive-experience-20082>.

14 eSafety Commissioner, 'Women in the spotlight: How online abuse impacts women's working lives', <www.esafety.gov.au/research/how-online-abuse-impacts-women-working-lives>.

15 Christie, R, 'The digital reputation report', *Propel Group*, 11 November 2023 <propelgroup.com.au/the-digital-reputation-report/>.

16 Christie, R, 'How women are speaking up on social media and winning', *Women's Agenda*, 3 May 2023 <womensagenda.com.au/latest/soapbox/how-women-ceos-are-speaking-up-on-social-media-and-winning/>.

17 Kramer, A, 'Why women face a sound barrier in their fight to be heard', *Forbes*, 11 December 2023 <www.forbes.com/sites/andiekramer/2023/12/11/why-women-face-a-sound-barrier-in-their-fight-to-be-heard/?sh=29477b814bc5>.

18 Sieghart, M, *The Authority Gap*, Penguin, 2021, p. 107.

19 Seighart, 2021, p. 117.

20 Spencer-Elliott, L, 'Of course calling women emotional undermines them at work', *Grazia*, 2 November 2022 <graziadaily.co.uk/life/in-the-news/calling-women-emotional-sexism/>.

21 Williams, J & Mikhaylo, S, 'How the best bosses interrupt bias on their teams', *Harvard Business Review*, November–December 2019 <hbr.org/2019/11/how-the-best-bosses-interrupt-bias-on-their-teams>.

22 Newman, C, 'Women helping women: Study shows promoting one woman helps many more', *UVA Today*, 11 December 2017 <news.virginia.edu/content/women-helping-women-study-shows-promoting-one-woman-helps-many-more>.

23 Ammerman & Groysberg, 2021, p. 157.

24 Diehl, A, Dzubinski, L & Stephenson, A, 'Women in leadership face ageism at every age', *Harvard Business Review*, 16 June 2023 <hbr.org/2023/06/women-in-leadership-face-ageism-at-every-age>.

25 Monash University, 'Study confirms English sounding names get more call backs from job applications than ethnic names', *Monash News*, 4 July 2023 <www.monash.edu/news/articles/study-confirms-english-sounding-names-get-more-call-backs-from-job-applications-than-ethnic-names>.

26 Sciacca, K, 'Why respecting pronouns matters', *Diversity Council of Australia news*, 17 July 2023 <www.dca.org.au/news/blog/respecting-pronouns>.

27 Brands, R, 'Why women are fighting an uphill battle on military language', *The Guardian*, 24 March 2014 <www.theguardian.com/women-in-leadership/2014/mar/24/why-women-are-fighting-an-uphill-battle-on-military-language>.

28 LinkedIn, 'The state of corporate jargon report 2023', LinkedIn Corporate Communications, 13 June 2023 <news.linkedin.com/2023/june/state-of-workplace-jargon-report-2023>.

29 Textio, 'The truth about bias in performance feedback', 15 June 2022 <textio.com/feedback-bias>.

30 Smith, D, Rosenstein, J & Nikolov, M, 'The different words we use to describe male and female leaders', *Harvard Business Review*, 25 May 2018 <hbr.org/2018/05/the-different-words-we-use-to-describe-male-and-female-

leaders#:~:text=This%20gives%20us%20a%20better,to%20describe%20
men%20was%20arrogant>.

31 Abel, M, 'Why female bosses get different reactions than men when they
criticize employees', *The Conversation*, 20 September 2020 <theconversation.
com/why-female-bosses-get-different-reactions-than-men-when-they-
criticize-employees-145970>.

32 Cameron, D, 'Lost words and hidden histories', *Debuk*, 24 July 2023.

33 VicHealth, 'Framing gender equality', *VicHealth*, 2018 <www.vichealth.vic.
gov.au/sites/default/files/Framing-gender-equality---Message-guide.pdf>.

**Chapter 6 – Leading differently: Disrupting jobs, careers and power
structures**

1 Hasan, M, '"What women owe men:" Kate Manne talks male entitlement,
women's electability problem, and how to feel about Kamala Harris', *Vanity
Fair*, 21 August 2020 <www.vanityfair.com/style/2020/08/kate-manne-talks-
male-entitlement>.

2 Chief Executive Women, '2023 CEW census', 26 September 2023
<cew.org.au/advocacy/2023-cew-census/>.

3 Jacobs, E, 'Female CEOs in the making?', *Financial Times*, 16 July 2023
<www.ft.com/content/8dbb42fb-2974-4a1e-b8d6-694d76ad8b27>.

4 Baker, J, & Wade, M, 'It's really bad: New numbers paint a bleak picture for
Liberal women', *Sydney Morning Herald*, 4 April 2023 <www.smh.com.au/
national/it-s-really-bad-new-numbers-paint-a-bleak-picture-for-liberal-
women-20230403-p5cxm5.html>.

5 Fox, C, 'Do we need to set targets to boost women executives?' *Company
Director*, 5 November 2021 <www.aicd.com.au/board-of-directors/diversity/
gender/do-we-need-to-set-targets-to-boost-women-executives.html>.

6 ANZSOG 'How do we make gender targets work', 15 February 2023
<anzsog.edu.au/research-insights-and-resources/research/how-do-we-make-
public-sector-gender-targets-work/>.

7 Gould, J, Kulik, C, & Sardeshmukh, S, 'Gender targets and trickle-down
effects: Avoiding the 'decoupling dynamics' that limit female representation
in senior roles', *Australian Journal of Public Administration*, vol. 82, no. 2,
18 January 2023 <doi.org/10.1111/1467-8500.12576>.

8 King, M, 'Gender expert – and director of inclusion at Netflix – says office
politics work only for men. To fix it, let's all start "spending our privilege" in
smarter ways', *Business Insider*, 5 March 2020 <www.businessinsider.com/
director-inclusion-at-netflix-office-politics-catch-22-for-women-2020-3>.

9 Gassam Asare, J, 'Why DEI and anti-racism work needs to decentre
whiteness', *Forbes*, 15 February 2021 <www.forbes.com/sites/
janicegassam/2021/02/15/why-dei-and-anti-racism-work-needs-to-
decenter-whiteness/?sh=1476e8f55886>.

10 Carruthers, T, 'We achieved gender parity in astronomy in just five years',
Science in Public, ASTRO 3D, 17 November 2023 <astro3d.org.au/we-
achieved-gender-parity-in-astronomy-in-just-five-years/>.

11 Carruthers, 2023.

12 Carruthers, 2023.

Chapter 7 – Elevating decisive women

1   Baird, J, 'If nothing can keep us safe maybe our raw rage will', *Sydney Morning Herald*, 4 November 2023 <www.smh.com.au/national/if-nothing-can-keep-women-safe-perhaps-our-raw-rage-will-20231103-p5ehea.html>.
2   Hooton, A, 'A woman's work: why the story of George Orwell's forgotten first wife still matters', *SMH*, 1 July 2023 <www.smh.com.au/national/a-woman-s-work-why-the-story-of-george-orwell-s-forgotten-first-wife-still-matters-20230529-p5dc3y.html>.
3   Makortoff, K, 'You have a responsibility': How Aviva's Amanda Blanc has promoted equality in UK business', *The Guardian*, 16 December 2023 <www.theguardian.com/business/2023/dec/16/aviva-amanda-blanc-gender-equality-uk-business>.

The end of delusions

1   Saini, A, *The Patriarchs: How men came to rule*, 4th Estate, London, 2023, p. 34.
2   Saini, A, p. 100.
3   Hooton, A, 'The forgotten wife', *Good Weekend*, 1 July 2023.

Bibliography

Ammerman, C & Groysberg, B, *Glass Half Broken: Shattering the barriers that still hold women back*, Harvard Business Review Press, Boston, 2021

Ferguson, K & Fox, C, *Women Kind*, Murdoch Books, Sydney 2018

Fine, C, *Testosterone Rex: Myths of sex, science and society*, Icon, London, 2017

Gillard, J, (ed), *Not Now, Not Ever: Ten years on from the misogyny speech*, Vintage, Australia, 2022

Orgad, S & Gill, R, *Confidence Culture*, Duke University Press, Durham, 2022

Saini, A, *The Patriarchs: How men came to rule*, 4th Estate, London, 2023

Saini, A, *Inferior: The true power of women and the science that shows it*, 4th Estate, London, 2017

Sieghart, M, *The Authority Gap*, Penguin Random House UK, 2021

Vijeyarasa, R, *The Women President: Leadership law & legacy women's lives based on experiences from South & SE Asia*, Oxford University Press, UK 2022

Index

Abbott, Tony 187
ABC 134, 190, 195
Aboriginal Career and
    Leadership Program
    (NSW public service) 112
abortion, access to 2, 189
accountability 160
Adamecz-Völgyi, Dr Anna
    128
affinity bias 89
AGSM (Australian Graduate
    School of Management)
    111, 115
    Emerging Indigenous
        Executive Leadership
        Program 112–13
Al Jazeera 134
    The Stream 134
Ammerman, Colleen 40, 101,
    102, 103, 117–18, 139–40
    Glass Half Broken 40
AMP 20, 87–88, 121, 136
Anderson, Aunty Pat 153
Aquino, Corazon 121
Ardern, Jacinda 11, 121, 212
Asian Leadership Project 48,
    162–63, 204
Astro 3D (Australian
    Research Council Centre
    for All Sky Astrophysics in
    3 Dimensions)
    gender equity case study
        175–77
Athena Swan 26
Australia Post 6, 9, 117, 190
Australian Board Diversity
    Index 15
Australian Constructors
    Association (ACA) 81
    Construction Industry
        Culture Task Force
        182–83, 201

gender equity case study
    180–83
Australian Financial Review
    95
Australian Graduate School
    of Management Program
    (AGSM) 77
Australian Human Resources
    Institute 77
Australian Labor Party 163
Australian National
    University (ANU) 23,
    119, 133
Australian politics
    candidate selection
        158–59
    gender standards 156–58
    glass cliff examples 57
    'good bloke syndrome'
        155
    'jobs for the boys' 90
    not-for-profit
        organisations 158–59
    'Teals' label 155–56
    women 5, 10, 12–13, 29,
        155–59
Australians Investing in
    Women 5, 159
Aviva 121, 206–207

Bachelet, Michelle 122
backlash to gender equity
    DEI initiatives, impact
        75–76 see also DEI
        (diversity, equity and
        inclusion)
    education on gender
        data 86
    effectiveness 65–66
    existence, denial of 68,
        89–90
    'false feminism' 64

gender bias, denial of
    80–81
gender pay gap 70–73
    hallmarks of 64–65
    leadership behaviours
        115
    male resistance to
        women's truth telling
        67, 79–80
    men as active allies to
        women 84–86, 90–93
    personal relationships
        and 68–69
    power imbalance 79–80
    realism, need for 8, 63
    reasons for 42, 65–66,
        81–82
    roadblocks to addressing
        76
    traditional attitudes 65,
        77–78
    women, from 68–69
    workplace, in 65–68, 70
    young men 67–68, 91
bamboo ceiling 48–49,
    162–63
Bandler, Faith 151, 154
Barbie 7, 8, 41
Barilaro, John 90
Barr, Joe 180, 181–82
Barra, Mary 121
Berejiklian, Gladys 46
Bickerstaffe, Katie 121
Black Lives Matter 75, 151
Blair, Eileen 187
Blanc, Amanda 121, 206–207
'the boss'
    assumptions/traditional
        beliefs 45–48
    sharing boss jobs 166–70
Boss magazine 95, 96
Boston Consulting Group 98

boys' club 88–90
Brady, Vicki 7, 136
Brands, Associate Professor
  Raina 144, 146
Branson, Richard 95
Brown, Brené 109–10
Bullock, Michelle 7
bullying 6, 9, 28, 59
Burke, Tarana 151
Burney, Linda 154
Burns, Ursula 121
Byrne, Matthew 77, 90, 91,
  115

Calkin, Simon 97–98
Cameron, Deborah 147
Cannon-Brookes, Mike 166
caring and domestic work 3,
  37, 39–40
  care economy 61, 192–94
  division of labour 40–41
  valuing 61–63
Carlyle, Thomas 97
the Case Centre 103
Cass-Gottlieb, Gina 7
Chaffey, Dr Lisa 198–99
Chai, Julie 48, 162–63,
  204–205
Chamorro-Premuzic, Tomas
  31, 127–28
Champions of Change
  Coalition 82, 179
Chaney, Michael 210
Chavez, Hugo 113
Chief Executive Women
  (CEW) 119, 152, 159,
  166, 192
Chowdhary, Shirley 158
Cilento, Melinda 14
Climate 200 155, 156
Coles 7, 85, 171, 172
Collins, Jim 95, 102
  Good to Great 102
Committee for the Economic
  Development of Australia
  (CEDA) 14
Commonwealth Bank
  Australia 72, 169
Community Support Services
  (CSS) 202–203
Confederation of British

Industry (CBI) 206
COP29 (Conference of
  Parties Climate Change
  Summit) 210
corporate empowerment
  trend 27–28
Counsel, Jane 99–100
COVID, impact of 3, 18,
  37–38, 192–93, 196
Crookes, Annabel 39, 181,
  182–83, 201–202
Curtin University 13, 133

Dalai Lama 113
Daniel, Annabelle 46–47
Danziger, Pamela 58
Davis, Professor Megan 153,
  185
decision-making groups *see
  also* leadership
  Australia, in 7, 12–14
  barriers for women,
    addressing 3–4
  CEOs and gender 9–10,
    13, 16, 17, 24, 44, 58,
    59–60, 73, 102, 135,
    160
  climate change forums 2
  domination by men 1,
    8–9
  'Drop to the Top' 10
  female trailblazers
    185–86
  leadership gender gap 2
  learning from decision-
    makers 200–201
  next generation 207–208
  perception and reality,
    gap 9, 18–20, 211
  political 5, 11–13, 121,
    155–58
decision-making process
  45–48, 189–91
  anger, channelling
    186–88
  convention, going against
    203–205
  decisions under pressure
    189–91
  domestic violence and
    47–48

empathy 196–98
gender stereotypes
  45–47
listening 191–94
risk appetite 50–52
speaking out 205–207
stress 47
timing 201–203
women setting the course
  61–63, 208–209
DEI (diversity, equity and
  inclusion) 29, 48, 75–80
  activism from men, need
    for 83–85, 152
  CEOs, power of 152
  consulting firms 98–99
  discrimination against
    ethnic names 142
  Indigenous business
    students 111–12
  Indigenous directors,
    numbers 15
  Indigenous scientists 132
  LGBTIQ+ community
    5, 15, 24, 49–50
  lip service 76–77
  modelling 152
  targets 176
Delaney, Kishaya 153–54,
  207–208
Deloitte Access Economics 5
disability bias 5
Diversity Council of Australia
  16–17, 142, 200
Diviney, Hannah 21
Dodd, Moya 64
Dutton, Peter 157

Edmondson, Amy 98
Ely, Robin 126
equal opportunity legislation
  11
Equileap
  *Gender Equality Global
    Report & Ranking* 175
Ericson, Karitha 18
European Central Bank 95,
  121
everyday sexism
  amplification technique
    138

band-aid advice 124–30
categories 80
confidence and 124–28
confrontation 123
conversational
    manspreading 136–37
gender labour and Queen
    Bees 84, 138–40
imposter syndrome
    129–30
interruptions 136–38
language of leadership
    143–48
meetings 136–38
messaging, getting it
    right 150
micro-aggressions 123
micro-interventions
    148–49
names, use of 140–43
nicknames 140–43
non-binary pronouns
    142–43
put-downs 137–38
self-help solutions
    124–25
social media strategies
    135–36
speaking out 131–34

Fair Work Commission 14
Farquhar, Scott 166
Fennessy, Adam 141
Fensome, Ali 21
Ferguson, Kristin 97, 119
Ferrera, America 41
50/50 The Equality Project
    134
Financial Services Institute of
    Australia 70
Financial Times 159
Financy Women's Index 29
FINSIA 73
First Nations women
    role models 151, 153–55,
    160–61
Fisher, Alexandra 108–109,
    116
Fitzsimmons, Professor
    Terence 106–108, 110, 116
Flecker, John 81, 180–81, 183

flexible workplace policies
    37–40, 43–44
    sharing boss jobs 166–70
Flood, Professor Michael 48,
    67–68, 74, 91
Ford, Professor Caroline
    25–26, 81, 132–33, 205
Foster, Lucy 168–70
Fox, Lindsay 90
Fox-Smith, Gavin 82
Fraser, John 88
FTSE Women Leaders
    Review 159
Funder, Anna 187, 213
    Wifedom 187

gender bias 2, 4, 35, 213
    ageism 54–56
    appearance 54–56
    community support for
        reduction 73–74
    denial 80–81
    male scepticism 68
    marginalised groups 5
    maternity discrimination
        36, 44
    parental status 41–42
    research 11
    stereotypes, addressing 44
    women and privilege
        170–72, 194–95
    women's capacity,
        scepticism 45
    women's words and
        speech patterns
        147–48
gender equity
    action for women's rights
        1–2
    advocacy for women's
        rights 1–2
    backlash see backlash to
        gender equity
    business case for 92–93
    case studies 173–83
    consulting advice 98–99
    COVID, impact 3, 18
    critical mass, impact 165
    data collection 23–24,
        27, 42
    economic benefits 5

fixing approach 27
    international 2
    men's attitudes to 69–70,
        85–86
    monitoring outcomes
        29–30
    over-optimism 9, 23–27,
        31, 35, 68
    progress toward 2
    quotas and targets
        163–66
    resistance to 4, 6, 32–33,
        67 see also backlash to
        gender equity
    targets and 'trickle down'
        effect 86, 163–66
    top-down and bottom-up
        practices 64–65
gender fatigue 22
gender loyalty 88–89
gender pay gaps 4–5
    audits 71–72
    denial 72–74
    flexible workplace policies
        39
    gender attitudes to
        70–71
    legal impediments 11
    'merit' argument 74
gender power gap 72
Gender Social Norms Index
    (GSNI) 11, 70
gender stereotypes 9, 25,
    68–69, 77–78
    feminine skills 41
    motherhood 44
gender washing 1, 4, 8, 9,
    18–20, 211
    inadequate gender
        policies 19–20
    International Women's
        Day 20–21
    rhetoric and reality gap
        20, 21–23
    selective disclosure 19
gendered violence 3
    traditional ideas on
        decision-making
        47–48
George, Alexis 121, 136
Gill, Rosalind 109–10, 126

Index

Gillard, Julia 41, 56, 57, 86–87, 117, 121, 187, 212
  misogyny speech 87, 184, 187
Gladwell, Malcolm 60
glass cliff 44, 57–59
glass-hours ceiling 37, 44, 62, 160
Global Gender Gap Index, 2023 2, 10
Global Institute for Women's Leadership (GIWL) 23, 108, 116, 119, 133
Goldgrab, Sheila 84
Goldin, Claudia 43, 185
Goldner, Sally 53, 91, 212
Grant, Stan 195
Grant Thornton
  2023 International Business Report (IBR) 18
Groysberg, Boris 40, 101, 102, 139–40
  Glass Half Broken 40
Gupta, Tarun 152

Handlin, Denis 116
Hartge-Hazelman, Bianca 29, 30
Harvard Business Review 103
Harvard Business School 98
  Race, Gender & Equity Initiative 40
Hasan, Mahan 156
Haslam, Alex 57
Hatch, Patrick 59
HBS 101, 102, 117, 118
  Race, Gender & Equity Initiative 101
Heidrick & Struggles 15
Henaway, Kat 111–13, 160–61
Herbert Smith Freehills 154, 207
Hermoso, Jenni 64
Higgins, Brittany 29
Holgate, Christine 6, 9, 117, 121, 190–91
Holmes, Elisabeth 94
Holmes à Court, Simon 155
homophobia 5
Howard, John 155

Hudson, Vanessa 59
'hungry judge syndrome' 47
Hutchinson, Dr Jacquie 104, 105

Impact Economics and Policy 34
IMPACTER 29–30
Implicit Leadership Theory 142
Innes, Laura 85–86, 171, 172
INSEAD 51, 119–20
International Women's Day (IWD) 20–22, 78–79
intersectionality 4, 5, 15, 16–17, 22, 48–50, 212
  diversity decrease 15–16
  gender and cultural assumptions 48–49
  leadership 48–50
  LGBTIQ+ community 49–50

Jakobsdóttir, Katrin 12
James Hardie 59, 116
Jenkins, Kate 29, 185
Jesuit Social Services, the Men's Project 48
Jobs, Steve 94
John Holland 180, 181–82
Johnson, Boris 116
Joyce, Alan 45, 58
Jumbunna Institute for Indigenous Education and Research 200

Kanter, Rosabeth Moss 95
Karpin, David 104, 120
Kean, Matt 194
Keating Labor government 104
Kelly 75
Kelly, Sean 38
Kewley, Professor Lisa 175–76
King, Dr Michelle 171–72
Korn Ferry 58
Kotter, John 95
Kulik, Professor Carol 73, 74, 86, 164–65, 172–73
Kumaratunga, Chandrika Bandaranaike 121

Kunze, Astrid 139

Lagarde, Christine 95, 121
Laing O'Rourke 38–39, 181, 201
Lambie, Senator Jacquie 5
Lattouf, Antoinette 195
Lawson, Francesca 21
leadership see also decision-making groups; decision-making process
  adaptive 161
  ageism 54–56
  alpha leader risk 116–17
  alternative models 113–14
  appearance 54–56
  authentic 108–109, 116
  backlash 115
  bad behaviour, tolerance levels 59–60, 115
  biases 98–100, 170–72
  capability frameworks 99–100
  case studies 102–103, 118
  casual banter 144–46
  CEOs 9–10, 13, 152, 159–60
  context 114–15
  'credibility deficit' 56
  criteria for executives 99–100
  cultural perspective 112–13, 161
  diversity and 94–98, 104, 113–14, 118–20
  double standards 61, 116–17, 139
  educational institutions 100–105, 110–15
  emerging leadership groups 110–12
  female role models 120–22
  financial acumen 52–54
  gender stereotypes surrounding 45–48
  gendered leadership models 98–102, 106–110, 117–18, 120–21

glass cliff 44, 57–59
Great Man syndrome
  96–97
images of 94
Indigenous and culturally
  diverse women
  programs 161
intersectionality 48–50,
  104
Karpin report 104–105,
  120
language of 143–48
masculine version 3,
  4, 94–99, 100–101,
  103–104
military jargon 144, 146
motherhood skills 36–37
performance feedback
  language 146–47
politics, in 5, 11–13,
  31–32
quotas and targets
  163–66
recruitment practices
  146–47, 160
risk appetite 50–52
role models and teachers
  115
soft skills 98
sport imagery 143
support networks for
  women 105–106
theories of 106–109,
  115–16, 142
underestimation as
  advantage 198–200
vulnerable 109–10
women and privilege
  170–72, 194–95
work-family conflict
  40–41
leadership gender gap 2,
  8–16
  barriers 3
  board directors 14–16,
  66, 73
  confidence and 127–28
  credibility gaps 56–59
  executive levels 73
  family-friendly policies
  40

glass cushions 56–59,
  170
music industry 22–23
NGOs 17
STEMM (science,
  technology,
  engineering, maths,
  medicine) 25–26
trust issues 45
women and privilege
  170–72, 194–95
'leadership gurus' 94
'leaning in' 27–28
Legena, Susanne 9
Leibbrandt, Professor
  Andreas 142
Liberal National Party 163
LinkedIn 135, 145
Lloyd-Hurwitz, Susan 66,
  78, 119–20, 121, 152, 166,
  173–75, 185–86
Looney, Bernard 206
Lyons, Libby 92, 206

Ma, Melissa 54
McCarthy, Gordon 189,
  203–204
McCarthy, Wendy 189–90,
  203–204
McGowan, Ruth 159
McGuiness 60
McKinsey 98
McNamara, Sally 36
Macquarie Bank 7, 121, 152,
  153
Maguire, Daryl 46
Malley, Alex 116
Manne, Kate 156
mansplaining 52, 53, 56, 84
Mant, Alistair 104–105
Marin, Sanna 12
Masella, Mi-kaisha 22,
  154–55
Matildas 7, 64, 214
Mauboy, Jessica 154
May, Theresa 57
Mayer, Melissa 117
Media Diversity Australia
  194–95
Meeks, Jordy 39
#MeToo movement 67, 151

Melbourne University 38,
  39, 113
Mihaylo, Sky 138
Miller, Amalia 139
Mirvac 66, 166
  gender equity case study
  173–75
Modelling Respect and
  Equality Schools program
  (MoRE) 48
Modestino, Alicia Sasser 56
Mohamed, Mona 202–203
Mohammed, Mariam 54
Moran, Naomi 121
More Voices, More
  Representation 20–21
Morris, Jennifer 158
Morrison, Scott 60, 78–79,
  116, 199
Mors, Marie Louise 51
Mostyn, Sam 61–62, 160,
  192–94, 214
Mulcahy, Anne 159
Multicultural Communities
  Council of NSW 17
Multiplex 81, 180, 183
Musk, Elon 45, 94, 116

Nair, Leena 159
National Community
  Attitudes Survey 2023 67
National Gallery of Victoria
  90
National Press Club 61, 192
Network Capability and
  Culture 18
NSW Government Religious
  Communities Advisory
  Council 16

Ocasio-Cortez, Alexandria
  113
Okonjo-Iweala, Ngozi 121
The 100% Project 85, 89, 171
O'Neill, Meg 7
Orgad, Shani 109–10, 126
Orwell, George 187

Pahari, Boe 87–88
paid parental leave (PPL 1, 4,
  34–36, 182

Index

impact on women 36–39
men and 38–39
transition from 39,
43–44
Pallotta-Chiarolli, Maria 208
Pathways to Politics 158
People Measures 85
Perkins, Charles 191
Perkins, Rachel 191–92
Peters, Tom 95
Pew Research Center 79
Plan International Australia 9
Pocock, Senator David 156
Politics in Colour 111
Porter, Michael 94
Price, Jenna 46
Price, Senator Jacinta 5
PricewaterhouseCoopers
conferences 110–11
Priestley, Angela 10
privilege and gender 170–72,
194–95
Productivity Commission 7
progress narrative 1, 33, 35,
210
debunking 30–31
proximity bias 38

Qantas 58, 72
Queensland University of
Technology 48, 67

racism 5, 16
Reilly, Julie 159
Respect@Work 29, 211
legislation 4, 29
The Reykjavik Index for
Leadership 44
Ribiales, Luis 64
Rippon, Gina 50
Risse, Leonora 127
Rizvi, Jamila 148
Roe v Wade 2
Rudd, Kevin 57
Ruppanner, Leah 39
Ruston, Anne 60
Ružbacký, Roman 79, 90
Ryan, Professor Michelle
23–24, 26, 28, 57, 108, 129,
163–64

Ryan-Weber, Professor Emma
176

Saini, Angela 205, 213
    The Patriarchs 213
Sandberg, Sheryl 28
Saujani, Reshma 129–30
    Girls Who Code 129
Scale Investors 51
Schwartz, Carol 158
Sciacca, Kath 142–43
sexism 2, 3, 4, 9, 16, 24
    benign 56, 80
    everyday see everyday
        sexism
    hostile 80
    interventions against
        82–83
    whistleblowers 87–88
sexual harassment 4, 28, 67,
87–88
    reporting decline 28
Seymour, Tom 111
Shine, Associate Professor
Kathryn 133–34
Sieghart, Mary Ann 56, 136
Silva, Miriam 121, 196–97
Sirleaf, Ellen Johnson 121
Smith, Professor Catherine
104–105
    'Diversity awareness
        in management
        education' 104
Smith, Professor Lisa Harvey
177
social movements
    diversity in business
        160–62
    new power models
        153–55
    radical flexibility
        166–70
    women and 151–53
    women in politics
        158–59
Sojo Monzon, Victor 113–14
Stefanovic, Karl 132
Steinem, Gloria 212
STEMMinist Book Club
205
Step Up 85

Sturgeon, Nicola 11–12
Sukarnoputri, Megawati 121
Swift, Taylor 7
Sydney University
    Australian Centre for
        Gender Equality and
        Inclusion @ Work 119
Sydney Writers' Festival 155
Szlakowski, Julia 87–88

Tate, Andrew 68
Team Global Express 9, 117,
121, 190
Telstra 7, 136, 164
terminology 5–6
Textio 146
Thinkers 50 119
Thodey, David 164
Thunberg, Greta 151
Tink, Kylea 156–57, 199–200
Tinsley, Catherine 126
Tottori, Mitsuko 121
Trump, Donald 113
Truong, Jack 59, 116
Turner, Sam 39, 49–50,
197–98

Uluru Statement from the
Heart 185
University of Alabama's
Culver College of Business
58
    'You're fired! Gender
        disparities in CEO
        dismissal' 58
University College London
31, 128
University of South Australia
73, 164
University of Technology
Sydney (UTS) 31, 111,
171, 187, 200

van der Veen, Catherine
168–70
Veiszadeh, Mariam 194–95
Vijeyarasa, Ramona 31–32,
187–88
Vincent, Dr Niki 42–43, 100,
105–106, 136, 167–68
Viva Energy 82

gender equity case study
177–80

Walters, Rosie 19
Watermark 15
Weckert, Leah 7
Welch, Jack 95, 96–97
Westpac 39, 99
Wiersema, Professor
   Margarethe 51
Wikramanayake, Shemara 7,
   121, 152
Wilkinson, Lisa 132
Williams, Joan 138
Wilson, Denise 159–60
Wolfers, Justin 56
Women in Economics
   Network (WEN) 127,
   131, 132
Women for Election (WFE)
   158

Women in Media 64–65, 131
Women in Mining 205–206,
   210
Women for the Voice 191
Women's Business 111, 160
Women's Community
   Shelters NSW 46
Women's Economic Equality
   Strategy 16
Women's Economic Equality
   Taskforce 4, 194
Women's Economic
   Opportunities Review
   194
women's networks 84–85
Women's World Cup
   (WWC) 2023 7, 64–65
Wong, Senator Penny 5
Wood, Danielle 7
Wooldridge, Mary 71, 72,
   167

working from home (WFH)
   37–38
Workplace Gender Equality
   Agency (WGEA) 4–5,
   13, 29, 71–72, 92, 167,
   183, 206
Workplace Gender Equality
   legislation 22
World Bank 12
World Economic Forum 10
World Trade Organization
   12, 121
Wyatt, Scott 82, 177–80

Xerox 121, 159

Young, Nareen 171, 200–201
Yousafzai, Malala 113, 151

Zuckerberg, Mark 94, 116